WHO RUNS FOR THE LEGISLATURE?

REAL POLITICS IN AMERICA

Series Editor: Paul S. Herrnson, *University of Maryland*

The books in this series bridge the gap between academic scholarship and the popular demand for knowledge about politics. They illustrate empirically supported generalizations from original research and the academic literature using examples taken from the legislative process, executive branch decision making, court rulings, lobbying efforts, election campaigns, political movements, and other areas of American politics. The goal of the series is to convey the best contemporary political science research has to offer in ways that will engage individuals who want to know about real politics in America.

WHO RUNS FOR THE LEGISLATURE?

Gary F. Moncrief
Boise State University

Peverill Squire
University of Iowa

Malcolm E. Jewell
University of Kentucky (emeritus)

Prentice
Hall

UPPER SADDLE RIVER, NEW JERSEY 07458

Library of Congress Cataloging-in-Publication Data

Moncrief, Gary F.
   Who runs for the legislature?/Gary F. Moncrief, Peverill Squire, Malcolm E. Jewell.
      p. cm.—(Real politics in America series)
   Includes bibliographical references and index.
   ISBN 0-13-026608-6
      1. Legislators—United States—States. 2. Legislative bodies—United States—States.
   3. Elections—United States—States. I. Squire, Peverill. II. Jewell, Malcolm Edwin.
   III. Title. IV. Series.

JK2488.M664 2000
328.73'073—dc21   00-058015

VP, Editorial director: Laura Pearson
Director of marketing: Beth Gillett Mejia
Editorial assistant: Beth Murtha
Editorial/production supervision: Kari Callaghan Mazzola
Prepress and manufacturing buyer: Ben Smith
Electronic page makeup: Kari Callaghan Mazzola and John P. Mazzola
Interior design: John P. Mazzola
Cover director: Jayne Conte
Cover design: Kiwi Design
Cover photo: Reprinted with the permission of Richard Hildreth

This book was set in 10/12 Palatino by Big Sky Composition
and was printed and bound by Courier Companies, Inc.
The cover was printed by Phoenix Color Corp.

Real Politics in America
Series Editor: Paul S. Herrnson

© 2001 by Prentice-Hall, Inc.
A Division of Pearson Education
Upper Saddle River, New Jersey 07458

Printed in the United States of America
10 9 8 7 6 5 4 3 2 1

ISBN 0-13-026608-6

PRENTICE-HALL INTERNATIONAL (UK) LIMITED, London
PRENTICE-HALL OF AUSTRALIA PTY. LIMITED, Sydney
PRENTICE-HALL CANADA INC., Toronto
PRENTICE-HALL HISPANOAMERICANA, S.A., Mexico
PRENTICE-HALL OF INDIA PRIVATE LIMITED, New Delhi
PRENTICE-HALL OF JAPAN, INC., Tokyo
PEARSON EDUCATION ASIA PTE. LTD., Singapore
EDITORA PRENTICE-HALL DO BRASIL, LTDA., Rio de Janeiro

For Claire and Stephen
and for Janet

CONTENTS

PREFACE

It seems that almost everything written about political campaigns in the United States focuses on the national campaigns for president and the Congress, or occasionally on statewide campaigns for governor. Granted, these are high profile campaigns with substantial money and media exposure. They are, however, but a very small part of the total number of campaigns in the United States.

Within any given two-year period, there are only about 470 elections for federal office: 435 for the U.S. House of Representatives, and 33 or 34 for the U.S. Senate (and, depending on the year, there is the presidential election). Even if all the states held elections for their constitutional officers (governor, lieutenant governor, attorney general, etc.) in the same year, the total number of statewide elections would amount to fewer than 300. But in any given two-year period, there are between 5,000 and 6,000 state legislative elections.

State legislative elections are increasingly important. As the tide of federalism ebbs away from the national government, its powers and responsibilities wash upon state shores. Today, state governments—and particularly the state legislatures—make important and often innovative policy decisions involving education, health care, social welfare, criminal justice, taxation, and many other issues.

Furthermore, state legislatures are a critical training ground for future national officeholders. Over half of the members of the U.S. Congress are former state legislators. Many, if not most, governors and other statewide officials previously served in the state legislature.

Unfortunately, state legislative elections today do not attract enough candidates. Incumbents often face no opposition. Potential challengers are scared off by the difficulties of a campaign against a better known, more politically experienced, well-funded incumbent. Even if there is no incumbent running, many qualified people do not want to undertake the very arduous task of campaigning.

Yet some people do make the decision to run. They cross the threshold from private citizen to public candidate. This book—*Who Runs for the Legislature?*—is about those people. It is not about the people who are already serving in the legislature. It is about the nonincumbents who run for office. Who are these people? Why are they willing to run? How did they come to the decision?

Our answers to these questions are based on a questionnaire survey of candidates in eight states, on personal interviews with candidates in three states, and on both a survey and personal interviews with party leaders in over half of the states.

A Boise State University (BSU) Faculty Research Grant helped pay for the questionnaires and travel to interview candidates. We wish to thank the Office of Research Administration at BSU for making these funds available. Amy Allen provided very capable research assistance at BSU.

Thanks also go to Paul Herrnson, Professor of Political Science at the University of Maryland, for his support and belief in this project. As editor of the *Real Politics in America* series, Paul demonstrated a strong and consistent vision and a quiet patience as he helped us mold the manuscript into this book. Beth Gillett Mejia, former Executive Editor for Prentice Hall's political science division and now Director of Marketing, has been very supportive and helpful; she is the consummate professional. Kari Callaghan Mazzola and John Mazzola handled the production process with skill; they were a pleasure to work with.

Finally, we thank the state party officials and the hundreds of candidates who took the time to complete our surveys, and we especially thank the many candidates, party leaders, and other experts who consented to personal interviews.

Gary F. Moncrief

Peverill Squire

Malcolm E. Jewell

Who Runs for the Legislature?

CANDIDACY AS POLITICAL PARTICIPATION

In the 1998 state legislative elections in Florida, Republican incumbent Carlos Lacasa had an easy time of it. No one ran against him in the general election. No one ran against him in the primary election, either. He did not so much *run* for reelection as he *cakewalked* to reelection. Perhaps Representative Lacasa was doing such a good job as state legislator that no one—Republican, Democrat, or Independent—was unhappy with his performance and wanted to see him replaced. Perhaps, but the fact is that 44 percent of all state legislative elections in Florida were uncontested in both the primary and general election in 1998.

Three thousand miles to the northwest, State Representative Celia Gould faced no primary or general election challenge for her District 22 seat in Idaho in 1998. Nor did she have opposition in 1996. The same for 1994—that's three straight elections with *no* electoral opposition at all.

Back across the continent in Boston, Shirley Owens-Hicks was elected to the Massachusetts legislature from District 6 of Suffolk County. No candidate ran against Owens-Hicks, yet almost 30 percent of the voters in District 6 chose not to vote for her; they left their ballots blank instead.

These are not isolated cases. Across the fifty states there is a high incidence of uncontested seats, races in which one of the two major parties can not find a candidate to run for the legislature. Over the past decade, roughly 35 percent of state legislative seats in the nation were uncontested in the general election.[1] This is almost three times the percentage of uncontested seats for the U.S. Congress.[2] In some states the situation is particularly severe. In 1996, for example, two-thirds of the seats up for election in Arkansas were uncontested. And the problem is not confined to the South. In Idaho, 50 percent of state house seats and 57 percent of state senate seats were uncontested in the 1998 general election. Obviously, in many places it is hard to get people to run.

Why should anyone care if no one runs for elective office? Under the U.S. Constitution, the American political system is a democratic, federal republic where citizens elect representatives to govern. Article IV, section 4, of the Constitution guarantees the states the same republican form of government as at the national level. Thus those who govern are to be chosen by the citizenry.

As a consequence, elections occupy a central place in the workings of our political system. Elections are the means by which citizens decide which people they want to govern and which policies they want enacted. The democratic system operates with an implicit expectation that elections will offer voters a choice between or among candidates, and by extension, between or among policy positions. Uncontested seats violate those expectations because they deprive voters of a choice. In this circumstance, the person who is elected to represent the voters is the person who opts to get his or her name on the ballot.

Thus, the American system of government needs people to run for office in order to give voters choices. The Constitution, however, is silent on such concerns. It makes no mention of any process by which potential candidates for elective office are to be identified or encouraged to run. Formal and informal processes to recruit potential candidates have evolved over time to fill this void. But, in many respects, the process remains mysterious. Who runs and why they decide to offer themselves for public service are critical questions to answer.

This book is about those who choose to run for the state legislature and how they arrive at that decision. It is also about candidate recruitment. Recruitment studies have a long history within the discipline of political science.[3] Almost all the studies, however, were done many years ago, and much has changed in the recruitment process since then. We aim to re-examine the recruitment process in light of today's new political realities.

We emphasize that this book is about the recruitment of *nonincumbent* candidates. Because so many incumbents run for reelection, the quality of the electoral choice presented to the voters depends greatly on the quality of the nonincumbents who are willing to challenge the incumbents or to run for open seats that have no incumbent running for reelection.

Why study the recruitment of state legislative candidates rather than candidates for national or local office? Understanding state legislative candidate recruitment is a particularly pressing need today because of four significant trends. First, devolution—the flow of policymaking power away from the national government and toward the states—is one of the important political forces in American politics. Increasingly, state governments are empowered to make many of our most important public policy decisions.

Second, within the policymaking nexus of the states, legislatures have become more important than they had been in the past. Many of the keenest observers of state legislatures recognize that they are vastly improved institutions. Today, they are far more capable of undertaking policymaking, setting the state budget, and overseeing the agencies of state government.[4]

Governors no longer dominate state politics; state legislators are powerful players too.

Third, there is a notion that as the institution of the state legislature changed over time, so did the sorts of individuals serving as legislators. Much has been written lately about the "new breed" of state legislators—young, bright, ambitious, and extremely capable individuals.[5] If, indeed, the type of person now serving in many state legislatures is different from the type of person who used to serve, then we might expect that recruitment processes also have changed along the way. We need to know not only *who* strives for the position of state legislator, but also *how* these individuals come to make the decision to run. These are fundamentally questions about political recruitment. The great variety of state legislative settings allows us to explore these questions in a depth not provided by virtually any other elective office.

Finally, the importance of who serves in the state legislature matters not only for state politics. It has implications for national politics as well. Service in the state legislature is an important springboard to office at the national level. In 1998, for example, over half of the members of the U.S. House of Representatives and over a third of U.S. Senators had previously served in state legislatures. Thus, many national leaders are drawn from state legislative ranks.

While this book is about recruitment of state legislative candidates, it also examines another issue of great consequence. It is a study of political participation in the most fundamental sense. There is substantial evidence that across a wide spectrum of organized activities, from bowling leagues to churches, Americans are less actively engaged than they used to be.[6] In many cases, participation is limited to writing a check. This is particularly true in regards to politics. Voter turnout rates have declined over the past generation. Americans are even less willing than they used to be to check the box on their tax forms that directs money to pay for the presidential campaigns, an act that costs individual taxpayers nothing. Thus, in recent years we have witnessed a decline in even the simplest forms of political participation. Noted one Colorado candidate during the 1998 campaign, "People aren't very interested in the system. People are ignorant about the system. It is very frustrating."

If organizations find it harder to get people to join and participation in most forms of politics has declined, it is also likely that the number of party activists at the state and local level has decreased and that people have less time to be active in the party. Moreover, it appears that a smaller proportion of the intelligent, hard-working people with some interest in public affairs are active in other kinds of civic clubs and organizations. Such a decline in participation in party and civic organizations would have substantial impact on the political system because these are the places where party leaders and others look for possible candidates. It may be, then, that the pool of potential recruits (at least the pool where recruiters traditionally look) may be smaller than it was in the past.

No greater commitment to participation in the political process can be made than to stand for election. Most Americans give little thought to what is involved in running for elective office. Unappreciated is the tremendous personal cost in money, time, and emotion involved in seeking public office. As one candidate told us, "That was *my* name on the campaign mailers and brochures. That was *me* knocking on the doors. It was *me* they were going to accept or reject on election day." Who decides to hazard a step into the political arena and the processes that bring them to that momentous decision is the focus of this book.

THE COSTS AND BENEFITS OF BEING A STATE LEGISLATOR

The idea of a citizen-legislator is a powerful one in American political life. The image of *Cincinnatus* leaving the farm to serve his country and then returning back home once the job was done is often applied to state legislators. The romantic ideal in many places is for people from a variety of ways of life to converge on the state capital for several months to meet as a legislature, and then for each of them to return to their regular professions once the session is over.

To some extent, citizen-legislators may well have been the norm for much of this century. Consider the conclusion about the type of individual serving in the state legislature drawn from a classic study written more than three decades ago:

> One gets the impression that though they are *in* politics, the bulk of these state politicians do not expect to live *off* politics or *for* politics. Their legislative career appears to be only a temporary episode in their total life space, to be cherished while it occurs, but an episode, even if protracted, nevertheless.[7]

Contrast that assessment with one of the contemporary political scene:

> What matters most … is ambition. Political careers are open to ambition now in a way that has not been true in America in most of this century. Those with the desire and the ability to manipulate the instruments of the system— the fundraising, the personal campaigning, the opportunities to express themselves in public—confront very few limits on their capacity to reach the top.[8]

On the surface, service in many state legislatures still appears to exemplify the citizen-legislator ideal. Pay is too low to support a family, but session lengths are short enough that they allow for the possibility of continuing one's main occupation. Yet the part-time appearance of legislative service, even in the lowest-paid, shortest-session legislatures, is probably superficial. Instead, legislators in many states get part-time pay for what is in essence full-time work. The phone calls, the speeches, the community meetings, and the requests by constituents for help of all sorts do not end when the gavel falls at the conclusion of a legislative session.[9] Service in every state legislature is demanding.

There are, of course, substantial differences in the pay structure across the fifty states. The annual salary in California is approaching $100,000 with a wide range of benefits. But only a handful of states are like California in that they pay enough in salary for someone supporting a family to contemplate service. In contrast, most states pay legislators minimal salaries of between $10,000 and $20,000, a level at which it is hard to support a family without some additional sources of income. And some states offer only a token sum—New Hampshire, for example, pays $100 per year—and little, if anything, in the way of health insurance, pensions, and other benefits. Thus, in most states, pay and benefits are too low for most people to justify taking time away from their "real" jobs to serve in the legislature. In New Hampshire, for example, women who do not work outside the home, students, and retired persons constitute a significant percentage of state legislators.

Legislative session lengths also vary enormously across the states. A number of states have short session lengths of thirty or sixty days, a few even meet only every other year. In those situations it may be reasonable for some people to take time off from their regular occupation to serve in the legislature. But most state legislatures meet for more than sixty days. The Maine state legislature, for example, meets for three-to-five days a week over a six-month period in the first year of the session, with a three-month session in the second year. For their labors, Maine legislators are paid a total of $18,000 for the two years of service. The state legislature in Iowa begins its annual session in January and usually wraps up business in late April or early May. Its members earn about $20,000 per year. And some legislatures, such as those in California, Massachusetts, and Wisconsin, meet year round, paying their legislators $99,000, $46,000, and $39,000, respectively.

The combination of pay and time demands generally limits who can serve in the state legislature. In the few well-paying states, full-time service is adequately compensated, but in most states, legislators are not paid enough to compensate for the time they lose from their other occupations. One successful lawyer serving in the Georgia state legislature, for example, claimed that he loses $50,000 a year from his law practice because of the hours he can not bill while he is in Atlanta serving in the legislature.[10] This problem has not escaped the notice of legislative leaders, party officials, and others who actively seek to recruit candidates to run for the legislature. The senate leader in Maine, for example, recently noted that during a speech to a group of business leaders in his state, "I explained how the Legislature was structured and what the compensation was, and I asked them how many could serve, and not one person raised their hand. This was in a roomful of about two hundred people to whom you would normally go to find your candidates."[11] A similar concern was raised by a Washington state legislator reflecting on the difficulties of recruiting people to run for that legislature. Pointing to one of Seattle's many office buildings, he lamented that there are

> a lot of young professionals and others in those offices there ... who have something to offer. How do you get them to come forward? If a company will say "We will offer this opportunity to everyone in the company" you could create a legislature of more skills. You'd have a bigger pool of talent ... *if they had some way to cover themselves financially.*" (Emphasis supplied.)[12]

It is hard to get people to sacrifice their careers and financial well being to serve in public office. The consequences of limiting the kinds of people who can serve in office are substantial. A New York state senator observed, "When you go full time ... you eliminate categories of people who can be legislators. A businessman can't be away from his shop this long. A young mother can't be away from her children this long. And every time you eliminate a category, you diminish the quality of the legislature."[13] The structure of legislative service in the states, in essence, imposes selection criteria on who can serve in office. Many people simply are not in a position to devote the time being a legislator usually requires or to accept the financial consequences of service. As one Georgia representative noted about the situation in his own state, "The legislature is beginning to get three groups: the rich, the retired and the broke."[14]

There is, however, another problem beyond financial calculations that limits interest in serving as a state legislator. There are also social pressures. In recent decades, both the public and the media have held elected officials in low regard. Indeed, in many cases running for office opens one to abuse from the electorate. One candidate in Washington state complained to us that during the campaign, "You get tired of people yelling obscene things at you, calling you a bitch, flipping you off." Occasionally a candidate must even endure physical threats. Take, for example, the plight of one candidate for the Oklahoma House of Representatives:

> Bill started receiving crank calls that were intended to discourage him from running. After he filed for election, the death threats started.... Then, in late July, while staking yard signs, a rock was cast from a passing vehicle that struck him in the back.... Two weeks later a minivan tried to run him down, again while placing yard signs.[15]

Not surprisingly, a Washington state legislative official active in recruiting candidates lamented to us that candidate recruitment is becoming more and more difficult because people just do not want to subject themselves to the nastiness of the campaign process and to the personal attacks.

THE HIGH AND EVER-INCREASING COST OF CANDIDACY

Candidates running for office incur many costs. Most obvious is the amount of money that has to be raised to finance a campaign. But there are other costs that also make becoming a candidate less than appealing.

The time involved in both campaigning for and serving in office often put severe strains on one's family life and finances. Campaigning for the state legislature has become a full-time vocation.[16] Hours, days, and months are devoted to meetings, speeches, knocking on doors, and a host of other campaign events. It is all consuming and candidates sacrifice time with their families and time at work.

Take, for example, the personal costs incurred by one 1998 challenger, a veterinarian, running for a seat in the Washington legislature. She observed that running for the legislature "takes the same sort of commitment that Vet School took—just not for as long." She started campaigning full-time in mid-June and ended up putting eighteen thousand miles on her car traveling around the district. The campaign was so demanding that, as she bemoaned:

> I can't remember anything from those five months. There is the feeling you should always be doing something else, something more. I discovered Tylenol PM or [I] would never have been able to sleep, worrying about what else I should be doing…. You just aren't there physically or emotionally [for your family] during the campaign process. The kids have to do the grocery shopping. My husband didn't realize how much the campaign would invade the home space—the telephone ringing constantly, etcetera.

Candidate after candidate we interviewed talked at length about the time they had to devote to the campaign. This is a problem that we will explore in depth in Chapter 4. A Colorado candidate's observation encapsulates the common experience: "I used to take the politicians' statements about how hard they worked with great skepticism, but I've never worked harder in my life than in this campaign."

Beyond the time commitment, however, campaigns also require money. Running for the legislature in most states has become an increasingly expensive proposition. In California, for example, candidates for the state assembly spend over $400,000 on average, with some races costing more than $1,000,000.[17] Among the candidates we interviewed in Washington state, it was not unusual for them to have raised $100,000 or more. Candidates in Alabama typically raised and spent somewhere in the range of $25,000 to $50,000, but there was wide variation depending on the nature and competitiveness of the district. In a few cases, candidates spent close to $100,000 for a house race and more for a senate race. The average figures in Colorado were slightly lower: in the $20,000 to $40,000 range. At the bottom of the scale, legislative contests in a few states, such as Maine, Wyoming, and Utah, cost only a few thousand dollars on average. Even these seemingly lesser amounts of money, however, represent a significant amount of time and effort in fundraising because candidates tend to collect money for their campaigns in $10 and $25 contributions. It takes a lot of little contributions to add up to a large campaign war chest. And candidates have to work hard to generate every donation.

Finally, nearly all candidates find fundraising the most distasteful part of the process. In particular, they dislike having to "cold call," that is, phoning people they do not know and asking them to contribute to their campaign. One Washington state candidate declared, "The money aspect is very distasteful.... I rebelled at begging for money." But successfully asking people for money has become a very big part of running for office. Not wishing to engage in it may well keep some people from seeking legislative office.

THE INCREASING DIFFICULTY OF GETTING CANDIDATES TO RUN

The picture painted of service in most state legislatures is not terribly pretty. The pay is low and the time demands are high enough that most people would have to leave their current employment in order to serve. Increasingly high campaign costs and the time and effort it takes to raise money also may discourage people from running. And finally, there are the statistical odds to face: When a challenger takes on an incumbent, the incumbent almost always wins. In 1994, for example, better than nine out of every ten incumbent state legislators who sought reelection were successful.[18] Overall, then, the appeal of being a state legislator is limited, the costs of running for the office are skyrocketing, and the chances of winning are low. This is hardly a good formula for enticing potential candidates to run for office. Given the seemingly dismal prospects of running for the legislature, rather than asking why more people do not become candidates, we might want to ponder why anyone chooses to run.

It is, of course, important to keep in mind that there are benefits to reap from running for office as well as from serving in office. One obvious potential benefit for any candidate is the possibility of winning. Indeed, it is even rational for long-shot candidates to make a race because the only way they can get elected to legislative office is to have their name on the ballot. And the probabilities are that (as nonincumbent candidates probably overestimate), once in a while, long shots pay off.[19] Moreover, by winning, one becomes a player in the policymaking arena. The opportunity to exercise power is, for many candidates, the key benefit of candidacy.

Another benefit may be ego gratification. Some people like the spotlight—to the extent that there is a spotlight in state legislative races. A candidate gets interviewed by the media and is often given the chance to speak to various community groups. A candidate's name and face appear on campaign brochures. Thus, there are psychological benefits that can prove to be a powerful attraction for potential candidates.[20]

Candidates also may obtain social gratification from the run for office. They meet other candidates, they meet party and elected officials, they meet volunteers active in party politics, and they meet prominent people in their community. In important ways, candidates often broaden their social networks.

Finally, some candidates run in order to influence public policy. They campaign to promote a specific policy position. It may be the right-to-life or the right to an abortion, or increased funding for public schools, or protecting the environment. State legislatures have considerable power over these and many other public policies. Even unsuccessful candidates may take comfort from the thought that they had the opportunity to influence public debate on many issues.

In spite of the potential benefits, however, in many districts in many states, nobody opts to oppose the incumbent legislators. Because competition is at the heart of American democracy, the incidence of uncontested races merits further examination (see Figures 1.1 and 1.2). The trend in uncontested seats for governors and the U.S. Senate, for example, looks much the same for the period between 1912 and 1998. Over time, the percentage of uncontested races declined and since 1964 virtually every election has been contested. Most of the seats that were uncontested prior to that year were in the South, where Democratic Party dominance often caused Republicans to concede without any fight. As the GOP became a more viable force in the South, fewer elections went uncontested. The trend for the U.S. House of Representatives also declined over time, although roughly 15 percent of seats have remained uncontested since the early 1960s.

FIGURE 1.1 UNCONTESTED ELECTIONS, 1912–1998: U.S. HOUSE AND IOWA HOUSE

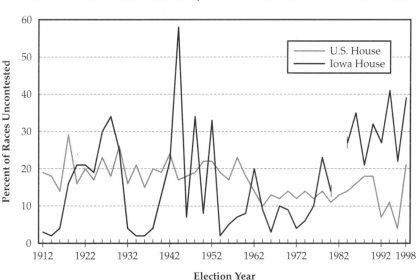

FIGURE 1.2   UNCONTESTED ELECTIONS, 1912–1998: SENATE AND GOVERNOR

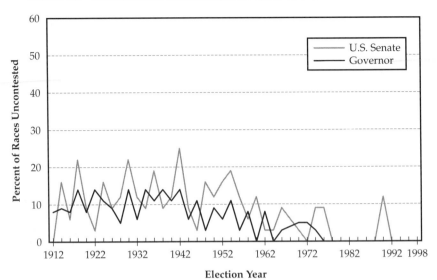

The picture for the Iowa House of Representatives contrasts markedly with those for the other offices (see Figure 1.1). In Iowa, the percentage of seats that go uncontested fluctuates over time, but since the 1960s, the unmistakable trend is an increase in the percentage of races where one of the two major parties fails to field a candidate. Obviously, only looking at one state is problematic; the pattern it reveals could be an aberration. But Iowa is a state celebrated for its strong civic culture.[21] Given its competitive two-party system and tradition of public service, the precipitous rise in the number of uncontested seats in Iowa is a glaring indicator of the larger problem: Over a third of all state legislative seats nationwide go uncontested.[22] And, unlike in elections for higher offices, the incidence of uncontested seats in state legislative elections is not dropping. It may even be increasing.

Differences in legislative structure and incentives have an impact on where state legislative races are likely to be uncontested. In Massachusetts, New York, and New Jersey, every seat was contested between 1992 and 1996 (see Table 1.1). A handful of other states also enjoyed high levels of contested seats. At the other end of the spectrum are Arkansas, Georgia, and Mississippi, where almost two out of every three seats had an absence of competition between the two major parties. Indeed, in six states, voters are more likely to find just one name on the ballot than they are to have a choice between two candidates.

The lack of electoral competition and voter choice brings with it some partisan advantage. In Arkansas, Hawaii, and Michigan, for example, the

TABLE 1.1 AVERAGE PERCENTAGE OF UNCONTESTED SEATS
IN LOWER HOUSE ELECTIONS, 1992–1996, BY STATE

STATE	PERCENT OF SEATS UNCONTESTED	PERCENT OF UNCONTESTED SEATS HELD BY DEMOCRATS	PERCENT OF UNCONTESTED SEATS HELD BY REPUBLICANS
Alabama	33%	77%	23%
Alaska	8	72	28
Arizona	19	29	71
Arkansas	67	91	8
California	4	44	56
Colorado	22	35	65
Connecticut	13	56	44
Delaware	32	44	56
Florida	48	52	48
Georgia	63	71	29
Hawaii	26	98	2
Idaho	45	18	82
Illinois	24	52	48
Indiana	30	46	54
Iowa	29	44	56
Kansas	22	52	48
Kentucky	58	75	25
Louisiana	25	72	28
Maine	15	64	36
Maryland	3	75	25
Massachusetts	0		
Michigan	4	92	8
Minnesota	7	21	79
Mississippi*	61	75	23
Missouri	34	62	38
Montana	27	51	49
Nebraska**	22	†	†
Nevada	7	33	67
New Hampshire	14	40	60
New Jersey	0		
New Mexico	49	68	32
New York	0		
North Carolina	28	61	39
North Dakota	10	40	60
Ohio	8	39	61
Oklahoma	45	64	36
Oregon	13	38	62
Pennsylvania	24	45	55

TABLE 1.1, CONT.

State	Percent of Seats Uncontested	Percent of Uncontested Seats Held by Democrats	Percent of Uncontested Seats Held by Republicans
Rhode Island	41	86	14
South Carolina*	56	54	46
South Dakota	14	34	66
Tennessee	43	63	37
Texas	56	62	38
Utah	20	20	80
Vermont*	12	56	42
Virginia*	30	47	49
Washington	14	45	55
West Virginia	21	84	16
Wisconsin	30	53	47
Wyoming	38	22	78

*One or more seats were only contested by third party candidates, thus percentages for the two major parties may sum to less than 100.
**Nebraska is a unicameral legislature; figures are for the one house.
†Nebraska elects its legislators on nonpartisan ballots.
Source: Data compiled by authors from Michael Barone, William Lilley III, and Laurence J. DeFranco, *State Legislative Elections* (Washington, D.C.: Congressional Quarterly, 1998). Data are averaged for the 1992, 1994, and 1996 elections years in all states except for Alabama and Maryland (1994 only), Louisiana (1995 only), Massachusetts (1994, 1996 only), Mississippi (1992 and 1995 only), New Jersey and Virginia (1993, 1995 only), and Vermont (1992, 1996 only).

Democrats enjoy virtually all of the uncontested seats. In Arizona, Idaho, and Utah, it is the GOP that benefits from the lack of competition. Clearly, the incidence of uncontested seats has a strong partisan edge to it in a number of states.

In some places, however, who benefits may be changing. Across the South, which was traditionally under the Democrats' control, the Republicans are often now the party that enjoys uncontested seats. In South Carolina, for example, in the 1992 election, Democrats had a 27-seat advantage over the GOP in the number of uncontested races. During the 1994, election that gap dwindled dramatically to a 6-seat Democratic advantage, and just two years later, the GOP actually enjoyed a 16-seat lead. The same turn of events occurred in Texas, and similar, although not as dramatic, trends were witnessed in Florida, Georgia, and North Carolina.

Why do some states host numerous hotly contested races while other states suffer so many uncontested elections? There are several reasons.[23] The pay for legislators varies substantially across the states and, not surprisingly, as member pay increases, the percentage of uncontested seats declines. But the explanation goes beyond just member pay. States also vary in their level of legislative professionalization,[24] which includes not only pay but also how long the legislature meets in session and the level of staff and other resources provided. The more professionalized the legislature, the more potential candidates value serving there, and the fewer uncontested races it hosts.

States also vary in their level of electoral competition. In states where partisan competition for elective office is keen, a lower percentage of seats are uncontested; in states where competition is lacking, higher percentages of uncontested seats are found. In the 1996 elections in Arkansas, for example, where the Democrats dominate, fifty-nine Democrats enjoyed uncontested races for the state House of Representatives, while only eight Republicans faced no opponent. Similarly, in Idaho where the GOP is supreme, the 1996 elections for the lower state house saw twenty-seven Republicans but only three Democrats with no opposition. Clearly, potential candidates for state legislative office behave rationally. They run where they have a good chance to win, and opt out of races in places where their prospects are dimmer. Thus, competition begets competition.

Finally, there is still less competition in the South than in the rest of the country. Uncontested seats for the Republicans have simply replaced uncontested seats for the Democrats. At the state legislative level, at least, region continues to matter.

Thus, from one perspective, candidates run where the value of the seat is high and where the electoral environment offers them a chance to win. But it would be a mistake to assume that the decision to run for the state legislature is a simple cost-benefit calculation. Candidates run for a variety of reasons. Take, for example, the explanations for running offered by two of the candidates we interviewed: A Colorado candidate said that he was being offered up as a sacrificial lamb in a race against a strong GOP incumbent. He recalled that during a local party meeting, "I opened my mouth and said somebody's got to do it—basically, I opened my mouth one too many times." The county chairman and house district chairman then leaned on him to become the candidate. A Washington state candidate, active in the party at the legislative district level, had tried to recruit someone else to make the race. He unsuccessfully canvassed the teachers' union, firefighters' union, and retirees for a potential nominee. When he could not convince anyone else to run, he decided that he did not want the incumbent to be unopposed, and he tossed his own hat into the ring.

OVERVIEW OF THIS BOOK

A basic tenet of most theories of democracy holds that voters should be given a choice between or among candidates for office.[25] Thus, it matters whether there are candidates for the state legislature on the ballot, and it matters who the candidates are. In Chapter 2, we examine the characteristics of the states that influence their different recruitment systems and the impact these systems have on whether candidates run for office. Then we look at who runs for the state legislature, using the results of a survey of nonincumbent candidates we conducted in 1997 and 1998 in Alabama, Colorado, Iowa, Maine, Michigan, New Jersey, Virginia, and Washington.[26] These legislatures were selected because they are in many ways representative of the fifty states. They are drawn from each region of the country, and they vary in terms of legislative professionalization, the number of women and minorities serving in them, and in the use of term limits. We supplement the survey data with a series of extensive personal interviews with candidates from Alabama, Colorado, and Washington. Taken together, the survey and interview information allows us to begin to understand who runs and why they come to make the race.

The agents of recruitment are examined in Chapter 3. Here we explore the roles different groups play in encouraging people to run for the state legislature, with particular attention given to state and local political parties, legislative caucuses, community and other groups, and non-traditional recruiters such as family, friends, and associates. In addition to drawing from our candidate survey and interviews, we use a survey of state party leaders to explain the recruitment process from their perspective.

Chapter 4 focuses once again on candidates. Using survey data and interviews, we look at the importance of the different social networks in which potential candidates contemplate running for office, and we explore in more depth the personal costs of campaigning for the state legislature. That approach is continued in Chapter 5 where we shift our attention to the state legislative candidacies of women, minorities, and third party candidates. Each of these groups has traditionally been underrepresented in state legislatures, although that may be changing. We compare the experiences of members of these groups to those of white males to learn whether there are systematic differences in their backgrounds or whether different recruitment processes and decision-making rules are at work.

We conclude in Chapter 6 with a final assessment of who runs and why they run—focusing particularly on how the candidate recruitment process has changed over time and what the consequences of these changes may be for larger issues in American politics.

Finally, one of the important features of this book is a series of *candidate profiles*, brief looks at some of the candidates we interviewed. There are ten such profiles interspersed throughout the book. The purposes of the profiles are twofold: to help drive home some of our points with true-life examples, and, more importantly, to help us see the candidates as real people. We end this chapter with the story of Billy John White (on pages 15–16).

☑ **BILLY JOHN WHITE**, Democratic candidate for the Alabama House District 11 open seat, 1998

A generation ago, Billy John White would have been a shoo-in for the District 11 election. A life-long Democrat, he lives in Baileyton, a small town about thirty miles south of Huntsville. The district is decidedly rural, mostly poultry farms and plant nurseries among the rolling hills of northern Alabama. The biggest town in the district is Cullman, with a population of about fifteen thousand.

White is the essence of the local southern politico of bygone days. He is a husky chain-smoker with a thick drawl, a polite and friendly manner, and an appealing low-key sense of humor. White attended the University of Alabama for three years during the 1960s but dropped out and went to work when he got married. He runs a tax preparation service from his home.

Billy John White has been around local Democratic politics for a long time. He served on the Cullman County Democratic Executive Committee for twelve years during the 1970s and 1980s. He also served as the city clerk for many years and was the assistant to the Cullman County commissioners for a while. He has waited a long time for this seat to come open. The previous officeholder—a Democrat, of course—held it for thirty years and was elected House Speaker twice. Obviously, one does not challenge such a local political institution, and White bided his time. "I guess I've been waiting for the incumbent to retire for some time," he said in his subtle, understated manner.

But over the course of those thirty years, the district changed. The power of the local Democratic organization declined and many of the voters who voted for the powerful Democratic incumbent were beginning to vote for Republicans for other offices. As White wryly observed, "I'm probably more liberal than most of the people around here. Of course, I'm not advertising that fact at the moment."

When the former speaker announced his retirement, the GOP targeted the seat for takeover. One good clue that the Republicans were confident they could win the seat is the fact that there were five candidates in the GOP primary. Billy John White was the only Democrat to run.

White received a little support from the Democratic party, but he also got help from the Alabama Education Association (AEA). The AEA and the Alabama Trial Lawyer's Association (ATLA) are two of the biggest players in Alabama Democratic politics—as are the Business Council of Alabama and the Alabama Farmer's Association on the Republican side.

White planned on five targeted mailings and some radio spots, but he was unable to procure the funding to do them all. As he said, "I have a lot of pledges for money but not enough actual cash has come in yet." In the meantime, "I do a lot of talking to local groups" like service clubs and organizations.

Billy John White was defeated; he received 44 percent of the vote, his Republican opponent received 50 percent of the vote, and a third-party candidate received the other 6 percent.

The Billy John White material is reprinted with the permission of Billy John White.

16

NOTES

1. Peverill Squire, "Uncontested Seats in State Legislative Elections," *Legislative Studies Quarterly* 25 (2000): 131–146.
2. The average proportion of uncontested seats for the U.S. House of Representatives between 1982 and 1996 was 12.6 percent, as calculated by the authors from data appearing in Table 1.1, p. 25, of Paul Herrnson, *Congressional Elections: Campaigning at Home and in Washington*, 2nd ed. (Washington, D.C.: CQ Press, 1998).
3. James David Barber, *The Lawmakers: Recruitment and Adaptation to Legislative Life* (New Haven: Yale University Press, 1965); Frank Sorauf, *Party and Representation* (New York: Atherton, 1963); and John Wahlke, Heinz Eulau, William Buchanan, and LeRoy Ferguson, *The Legislative System* (New York: John Wiley & Sons, 1962).
4. Alan Rosenthal, "The Legislature: Unraveling of Institutional Fabric," in *The State of the States*, 3rd ed., ed. Carl Van Horn (Washington, D.C.: CQ Press, 1996), 109.
5. See, for example, Alan Ehrenhalt, *The United States of Ambition* (New York: Random House, 1991); Alan Rosenthal, *The Decline of Representative Democracy* (Washington, D.C.: CQ Press, 1998); Peverill Squire, "Another Look at Legislative Professionalization and Divided Government in the States," *Legislative Studies Quarterly* 22 (1997): 417–432; and Joel A. Thompson and Gary F. Moncrief, "The Evolution of the State Legislature: Institutional Change and Legislative Careers," in *Changing Patterns in State Legislative Careers*, ed. Gary F. Moncrief and Joel A. Thompson (Ann Arbor: University of Michigan Press, 1992).
6. Robert Putnam, "Bowling Alone: America's Declining Social Capital," *Journal of Democracy* 6 (1995): 65–78.
7. Wahlke, Eulau, Buchanan, and Ferguson, *The Legislative System*, 134.
8. Ehrenhalt, *The United States of Ambition*, 272–273.
9. On this point, see political scientist Frank Smallwood's account of his service in the Vermont state legislature. Frank Smallwood, *Free and Independent* (Brattleboro, Vt.: The Stephen Greene Press, 1976).
10. Dana Milbank, "A House Divided: Part-Time Legislators Ask: Should We Make Laws or Make A Living?" *Wall Street Journal*, January 8, 1997, p. A1.
11. Sandor M. Polster, "Maine Panel to Consider Legislative Reform," stateline.org, 6 July 1999.
12. Richard W. Larsen, "Jim McDermott Reflects on Washington State Politics," *Seattle Times*, 20 July 1987.
13. Emanuel R. Gold quoted in Jeffrey Schmalz, "In Albany, They Can't Stop Meeting," *New York Times*, 31 July 1988.
14. Georgia State Representative Mike Snow quoted in Dana Milbank, "A House Divided: Part-Time Legislators Ask: Should We Make Laws or Make A Living?"
15. Ronald Keith Gaddie, "The Hopes Which Lie in Hearts of Young Men Part 1: The Origins of Political Ambition" (Paper prepared for the Annual Meeting of the Southwestern Political Science Association, San Antonio, Tex., March 1999), 14.
16. Ehrenhalt, *The United States of Ambition*. On this point see Bruce Altschuler's campaign diary of a political science colleague's campaign for the New York state assembly. Note the great amount of time the candidate gives to the campaign, time taken at the expense of family and profession. Bruce Altschuler, *Running in Place: A Campaign Journal* (Chicago: Nelson-Hall, 1996).
17. See Gary F. Moncrief, "Candidate Spending in State Legislative Races," in *Campaign*

Finance in State Legislative Elections, eds. Joel A. Thompson and Gary F. Moncrief (Washington, D.C.: CQ Press, 1998), 43.

18. These figures are from the National Conference of State Legislatures. See http://www.ncsl.org/programs/legman/elect/incmb1.htm

19. Jeffrey Banks and D. Roderick Kiewiet, "Explaining Patterns of Candidate Competition in Congressional Elections," *American Journal of Political Science* 33 (1989): 97–1015.

20. See Thomas A. Kazee, "The Decision to Run for the U.S. Congress: Challenger Attitudes in the 1970s," *Legislative Studies Quarterly* 5 (1980).

21. See Samuel C. Patterson and G. Robert Boynton, "Legislative Recruitment in a Civic Culture," *Social Science Quarterly* 50 (1969): 243–263; and Peverill Squire, "Iowa and the Drift to the Democrats," in *Party Realignment and State Politics*, ed. Maureen Moakley (Columbus: Ohio State University Press, 1992).

22. Squire, "Uncontested Seats in State Legislative Elections."

23. Squire, "Uncontested Seats in State Legislative Elections."

24. Peverill Squire, "Legislative Professionalization and Membership Diversity in State Legislatures," *Legislative Studies Quarterly* 17 (1992): 69–79; and Squire, "Uncontested Seats in State Legislative Elections."

25. Robert A. Dahl, *A Preface to Democratic Theory* (Chicago: University of Chicago Press, 1956); and Anthony Downs, *An Economic Theory of Democracy* (New York: Harper & Row, 1957).

26. In the summer of 1997, we sent a four-page questionnaire to nonincumbent candidates running for state legislative office in New Jersey and Virginia, the only two states to hold legislative elections that year. In the spring, summer, and fall of 1998 we sent surveys to nonincumbent candidates in six more states: Alabama, Colorado, Iowa, Maine, Michigan, and Washington. There were too few contested senate seats to survey in Virginia, so only candidates for the House of Delegates are included. Because of the very large number of candidates running in Michigan—over 500 were on the primary ballot—we sampled 120 candidates to survey. The overall response rate was approximately 50 percent, ranging from a low of 40 percent in Maine to a high of 67 percent in Iowa. The response rate was over 50 percent in Colorado, Iowa, Washington, and Virginia.

In the survey, we asked questions about the candidate's decision to run, such as when the decision was made and whom the candidate talked to before the decision was made. We asked about previous political activity including prior elected or appointed offices held. We also inquired about the respondent's assessments of his or her abilities in terms of fundraising, public speaking, and generally managing a campaign. Finally, we sought information about his or her personal backgrounds; such as race, gender, age, and education.

THE CONTEXT OF RECRUITMENT AND CANDIDACY

In this chapter we ask, "Who runs for the state legislature, and why?" We rely on information from surveys and interviews to provide some general answers to these questions. It is important to recognize that the answers can be a little different from one state to another because the political environment is not the same from state to state.

VARIATIONS IN RECRUITMENT PATTERNS

Candidate recruitment is a product of many variables. These factors include the nature of the political system in a state (*systemic variables*), the political conditions in the legislative district in which the election is to be contested (*district variables*), and the individual attributes and decision-making calculus of the potential candidates themselves (*individual variables*). All these variables may enter into the determination of who runs for legislative office (see Table 2.1 on page 20).

DIFFERENCES IN STATE POLITICAL SYSTEMS

Candidates for the fifty state legislatures run under fifty different sets of rules. Each state has a rather unique combination of electoral rules that define such important issues as how candidates get on the ballot, how they can raise money for the campaign, and when the primary election will be held. We call these *systemic* variables because they differ from one state political system to another.

The Nature of the Nominating System In most political systems around the world, the political party as an organization has the power to determine which potential candidates will serve as their nominees. That used to be the

TABLE 2.1   A COMPARATIVE FRAMEWORK FOR THE STUDY
OF STATE LEGISLATIVE CANDIDATE RECRUITMENT

SYSTEMIC VARIABLES	DISTRICT VARIABLES	INDIVIDUAL VARIABLES
• Type of nominating system	• Presence or absence of an incumbent	• Previous political experience
• Level of legislative professionalization	• Role of local support group	• Personal resources
• Electoral opportunity structure	• District magnitude	• Career goals
• Campaign finance system	• Electoral geography	• Gender
• Level of party competition and strength	• District marginality	• Racial/ethnic background
• Political culture		
• Term limits		

case in many states in this country as well. A few decades ago, for example, political party bosses in Connecticut held almost complete control over the nomination process.[1]

Such unfettered power is no longer evident anywhere in the United States. The role of parties in the nomination process is now more complicated, in large part because of the introduction of direct primaries. Some nominating systems, such as open primaries, blanket primaries, and nonpartisan primaries, impose few constraints on who can seek a party's nomination, and as a consequence they greatly hamper the ability of the political party to nominate the candidate of its choice. Ultimately, it is the people who vote in the primary who make the nomination decision, not party leaders. Other systems, particularly closed primaries and district conventions, give a state party a greater opportunity to influence the outcome of the nomination process.

Historically, parties were more active in recruiting and supporting candidates in those states with more restrictive nominating systems such as Connecticut and Pennsylvania than in states with more open primary election systems, such as Washington and Minnesota.[2] In other words, the type of primary election affected the role of the political party in recruitment. This relationship between primary type and the recruitment role of the party may not be quite as strong today, but it still exists. Open primary systems provide more room for individual candidate initiative and less control for the political parties.

A few states still have a procedure allowing the party to endorse a specific candidate prior to the primary. As one would expect, the endorsed candidate wins most of the time.[3] The ability to explicitly endorse individual candidates strengthens the role of the party in the nomination process.

Colorado is among the few states where parties still employ a caucus system to determine nominations. Both parties in that state use precinct caucuses to select delegates to the county assembly, which in turn puts nominees on the primary ballot. Candidates make it onto the primary ballot if they get 30 percent of the votes in the assembly. This caucus system gives party leaders a good deal of influence over their party's nominations. Indeed, their influence can be particularly significant given the realities of caucus participation; in some cases only a handful of people attend their caucus. Such poorly attended precinct caucuses are almost always meetings of the minority party caucus in a district. Where few people participate, party leaders can exert their influence.

There are limits to that power, however. Even candidates who do not get the required 30 percent of the vote in the assembly can still get on the ballot by petition, which requires collecting several hundred signatures in support. A few candidates get on the primary ballot by this process—a loophole which reduces a party's power over nominations. In addition, it is possible for organized interest groups to stack a caucus, and ultimately the assembly, with their members in order to get their preferred candidate nominated. In Colorado, for example, religious right organizations have succeeded in doing this in GOP caucuses in some districts. Thus, even a system that appears advantageous for party leaders can instead be exploited by groups outside the parties or by specific factions within the party.

Different nomination processes attract different sorts of people as candidates. In some states, self-starters can seek the nomination on their own initiative without any prior party experience or even consultation with party leaders. In other states, parties wield greater control over their nominations and the candidates whose names get on the ballot would be more apt to be actively recruited by leaders. In this situation, candidates are more likely drawn from the ranks of party activists.

Legislative Professionalization   As defined in terms of members' salaries, level of staffing, and length of the legislative session, states vary in terms of legislative professionalization (see Figure 2.1 on page 22).[4]

Only a handful of states can be considered fully professionalized in the sense that their legislatures meet most of the year, the legislators are well paid, and the institution is well staffed. Generally, legislatures in the more populous states like California, Michigan, and New York fall into this category. A few other states, such as New Jersey and Florida, are well on the way to professional status. Most states, however, look little like the highly professionalized U.S. Congress. Indeed, they only faintly resemble the more professionalized state legislatures. Many legislatures are like those at the very bottom of the rankings, states that pay their legislators very little, do not have long sessions, and provide very little in the way of staff or other resources.

Salary is an especially important component that can alter the recruitment landscape.[5] For example, a Colorado legislative leader told us that there seemed to be a lot more people running for the state legislature in 1998 than in previous years because there was a substantial increase in salary—from

$17,500 to $30,000—beginning with the 1999 legislative session. Money gives at least some people an incentive to run. One Colorado candidate, a single parent, said "I couldn't run before because the $17,500 was too low." Only with the increase in pay could she afford to serve.

FIGURE 2.1   LEGISLATIVE PROFESSIONALIZATION

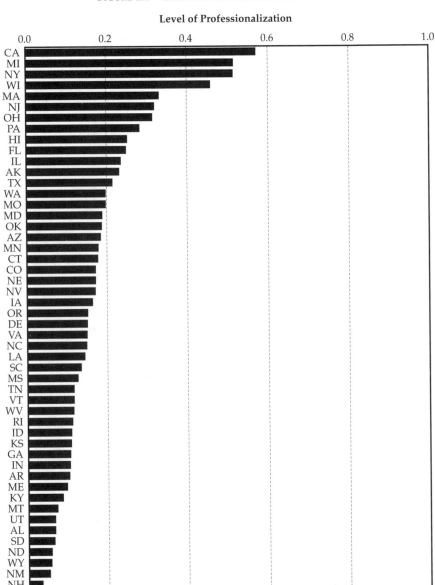

More highly professionalized state legislatures are also often associated with intense party competition for control of the chambers, motivating the parties or the state legislative leadership to be very active in the recruitment process. Legislative campaign committees, for example, are more active in professional legislatures than they are in less professionalized bodies.[6]

Finally, legislative professionalization may have a differential effect on the recruitment patterns of Democrats compared to Republicans. Some contend that Republicans find full-time legislative service less enticing because they must usually give up lucrative professional positions in the private sector to serve in a full-time, professional state legislature.[7] Moreover, there are still fewer women serving in the more professionalized legislatures than in the other state legislatures.

The Electoral Opportunity Structure Each state has a particular electoral opportunity structure available to potential candidates. This opportunity structure is based on the number of seats available in the legislature, the number of congressional seats from that state, and the number of statewide elected offices. It is also dependent, in part, on the nature of party competition, both nationally and within the state. Pennsylvania, for example, has a comparatively large state legislature (203 seats in the lower house and 50 state senate seats), 21 seats in the U.S. House of Representatives, 2 seats in the U.S. Senate, and 5 statewide elected offices (governor, lieutenant governor, secretary of state, etc.). In contrast, Nevada has comparatively few electoral opportunities: 42 seats in the state house of representatives; 21 seats in the state senate; 2 U.S. House seats, 2 U.S. Senate seats; and 6 statewide offices.

State legislative career patterns and membership turnover rates are influenced by opportunity structures in each state.[8] Specifically, different types of state legislatures are associated with different types of political ambition, which in turn affects the kind of person who is attracted to run for the state legislature. *Discrete* ambition is the desire to serve for just a few years in office, then return to private life. This is the essence of the "citizen legislator" who serves for a term or two and then chooses not to run again. It is, presumably, the type of political ambition that term-limit proponents favor. *Static* ambition is the desire to serve in the same office for many years; many state legislators truly enjoy the "legislative life" and have no desire to retire or run for another office. These people are often very loyal to the *institution* of the legislature. About 10 percent of state legislators nationwide have served in the same office for fifteen years or more. Then there are those who exhibit *progressive* ambition, seeking to move up the ladder of political offices. They often begin in locally elected office like city council or county commissioner, then serve for a few years in the state legislature before finding an opportunity to run for federal or statewide office.

Those who exhibit static or progressive ambition exhibit careerist orientations; both types of individuals seek a long-term career in public office. The difference between the two types is that one wants a long-term career in a specific office like the state legislature and the other wants a long-term career characterized by upward mobility.

The type of state legislature and the array of offices available in a particular state will aid or thwart these different types of political ambition. For example, the California legislature consists of 120 members (80 in the assembly, 40 in the senate). At the same time, there are about 60 statewide and congressional seats available in California. In other words, for every "higher" office (federal or statewide) elected from California, there are but 2 state legislators. In New Hampshire, on the other hand, there are 424 state legislators (400 house members, 24 senators) but fewer than 10 statewide and federal offices. In other words, there are 42 state legislators for every "higher" office elected from New Hampshire. Clearly, not very many New Hampshire legislators can seriously entertain progressive ambition. In California, though, state legislators have a very real chance to move up the political ladder.

The Campaign Finance System   The costs of candidacy for the legislature vary enormously by state.[9] The differences in costs are partly associated with differences across the states in campaign finance laws. For example, a few states like Wisconsin and Minnesota offer some public funding to candidates if they agree to limit their spending on the campaign. Some states limit the amount of money that a donor can contribute to any specific candidate to several hundred dollars, but in other states there is no limit at all—an individual or PAC can donate as much money as they want to a candidate. The differences from state to state in such regulations may affect a prospective candidate's assessment of how competitive he or she can be in the election and, therefore, whether he or she decides to run.

Changes in campaign finance laws may have consequences for candidate availability. Maine's new campaign finance law allows for full public funding of state legislative candidates who meet a very minimal vote share threshold. This law, if it withstands court challenges, is expected to encourage more candidates to file for state legislative office—including more independent and third party candidates.[10]

Calculating the likely effects of changing rules is, however, problematic, as the recent changes in Colorado's campaign finance rules show. The voter-passed Measure 15 limited the contributions of individuals and political action committees to $200.[11] Will such limits make it more or less likely that potential candidates will opt to make the race? Candidates in the 1998 race—the first covered by the law—sent mixed signals on this question. Several Democratic candidates preferred operating under the new law, liking that "you don't have to ask people for much money because you legally can not," and that "now you can't be buried by money." Such comments lead us to think that future candidates may be encouraged to run by the reforms. But the observations of other candidates suggest otherwise. One experienced Democratic candidate said, "Measure 15 has been just horrendous" because it makes fundraising so much more difficult. A GOP candidate concurred, noting that the reform "makes it dang hard to raise money."[12]

Competitiveness of the Political Parties Recruitment patterns are different in states with competitive political parties than they are in states in which one party is substantially weaker than the other party. A competitive party system means both parties have a legitimate chance to lead the legislature, depending on the outcomes in any given election year. A legislative seat is more attractive to a potential candidate if his party has a chance to be the majority in the legislative chamber.[13] Thus, the ability to recruit candidates differs depending on the relative strength of each political party within a state.

Tied to the competitiveness of the parties are issues of party leadership and the organizational strength of the parties. As a former Speaker of the Wisconsin Assembly put it, "In some states the political party recruits candidates and provides campaign help and money. In other states the candidate for the legislature is pretty much on his or her own."[14] While conventional wisdom is that parties have less control over the recruitment process today than in the past, there is growing evidence that in some states party officials are increasingly active in recruiting candidates.

Several legislative leaders told us that recruitment is becoming a higher priority than it had been in the past. Typical is a comment by the Speaker in one western state legislature, "Recruiting is very important.... Two of my deputy leaders take responsibility for each of the regions and interview prospective candidates from those areas." The majority leader in another state legislature said, "Recruitment is a high priority for me. I have designated eight regional campaign coordinators from my caucus covering the entire state. I meet with them at least once a month, often by conference call, to discuss our progress."[15]

Political Culture One of the most important characteristics that distinguish states from one another is political culture.[16] No one, for example, would confuse the reserved and low-key politics in Iowa with the rough-and-tumble partisan politics in Illinois.

One of the ways in which the recruitment process has changed in the past generation is that many of the barriers to holding office have been eliminated for women and racial and ethnic minorities. Inequalities remain, however. Several studies, for example, show that women are underrepresented in states where conservative Protestant or Catholic religious affiliation is high.[17] And fewer women hold legislative office in the more traditional southern states than they do elsewhere. Thus, the political cultures found in some states may be more open to the recruitment of a variety of people than are the cultures found in other states.

Term Limits   By the close of the twentieth century, term limits were in effect in eighteen state legislatures. Will term limits alter recruitment patterns?
It probably depends on the particular conditions of the term limit: whether the
limits are a lifetime or a consecutive year limit, and the number of terms permitted under the limits.[18]

Term limits clearly weigh heavily on the minds of potential candidates.
One Colorado legislative leader commented that there seemed to be a lot more
people running in 1998 than in previous years, which she attributed to the fact
that term limits created more open seats. At least one Colorado candidate, who
had run a credible race against a popular incumbent in 1992, said that he waited to run again until 1998 when term limits opened the seat; his odds of winning improved once the incumbent was forced out. Another Colorado
candidate noted that at first he was opposed to term limits, but later changed
his mind because, "People like me can anticipate an open seat and prepare."
The existence of term limits alters the calculations of at least some potential
candidates.

LEGISLATIVE DISTRICT CHARACTERISTICS

The particular political context of the legislative district can have a major impact on the decision making of potential candidates. These individuals consider many factors associated with the district.

Presence or Absence of an Incumbent   One of the important determinants
of the field of contestants in any given election is whether or not there is an
incumbent in the race. The advantage of incumbency in American elections,
including state legislative elections, is well documented. First, they have an advantage in name recognition. While it is true that even incumbent state legislators are often not well known among their constituents, any name
recognition is better than none at all. And most nonincumbent state legislative
candidates have virtually no name recognition.

Second, incumbents have campaign experience. Unless they were appointed to fill an unexpectedly vacant legislative seat, incumbents have already been elected at least once. They know what is involved in running for
office, they know how to organize a campaign, and it is an easy matter for
them to reassemble a campaign organization.[19]

Third, incumbents usually enjoy a substantial campaign finance advantage. In most states, challengers attract less than half as much money as incumbents can.[20] In the 1996 California legislative races, incumbents outspent
challengers by eighteen to one.[21] Part of the reason incumbents can spend so
much money is because they can attract a lot more money from interest group
PACS (political action committees) since they are already known to those
groups. Incumbents are often so well funded that they simply scare off most
challengers. The fact of the matter is that when an incumbent state legislator
faces an electoral challenge, the incumbent wins about 90 percent of the time.[22]

Challengers, therefore, face an uphill battle. Most of them have never held elective office, and many of them get into the race without a clear picture of what is involved. It is often a tough lesson learned. One of the challengers we interviewed in Alabama seven weeks before the election was upbeat and very confident of his ability to pull off a victory against a House incumbent. In late October, just one week before the general election, we checked in with him, asking how the campaign was going and what recent developments had occurred. His e-mailed response was succinct: "I just have one thought. What possessed me to do this?" A week later, the incumbent beat him by 26 percentage points.

Because incumbents are so hard to defeat, potential candidates often wait for an open seat. Open-seat races are generally more competitive, with each candidate having a better chance to win than if they were to challenge an incumbent. Without an incumbent in the race to draw off most of the campaign contributions, open-seat contestants can generally attract more money in order to run a credible race.

In some states, as many as 40 to 60 percent of incumbents run unopposed.[23] To put this another way, potential candidates are wary of the advantages of incumbency. A good example is the fact that members of the lower chamber in a state legislature rarely run against incumbents in the state senate. Instead, they strategically wait for the senate seat to become open before they run.[24] As a result, they are generally successful in winning the open seat.

Role of Local Support Groups   Local political party organizations became more active in recruiting state legislative candidates in some places during the 1980s and 1990s.[25] Local interest groups can be an important source of candidate recruitment and support. Groups such as the Farm Bureau, the Cattlemen's Association, and the local Chamber of Commerce were important sponsors in some rural legislative districts in Oregon in the 1960s.[26] More recently, the teachers' union is an important recruiter of candidates in Alabama and some other states.[27] In 1998, the Church of Latter Day Saints (Mormons), a particularly important force in Utah and parts of Idaho and Arizona, issued a letter to its church leaders and congregations, encouraging church members "to be willing to serve on school boards, city and county councils and commissions, state legislatures and other high offices."[28]

District Magnitude   State legislatures differ in district magnitude, or the number of legislators elected from each district. Most states use single member districts, where only one legislator is elected from each district. But some states use multimember districts, where two or three legislators are elected from the same district. The incumbency advantage in multimember districts is somewhat less than for incumbents in single member districts.[29] If incumbents in multimember districts are more vulnerable than they are in single member districts, stronger challengers are more likely to emerge. And, because of electoral self-interest, incumbents in multimember districts are likely to take a strong role in recruiting candidates to run with them as part of the party "team" in the district.

Electoral Geography   The size and demographic characteristics of some electoral districts influence who runs and how well they do.[30] For example, racial or ethnic minority groups hold a larger share of seats in lower chambers than in upper chambers, partly because house districts are smaller than senate districts, and the minority group is more likely to constitute a larger proportion of the district population in lower house districts.

The size of the district is also the biggest factor in explaining campaign costs in state legislative districts.[31] Districts with more eligible voters usually have higher campaign costs, which will discourage less-wealthy potential candidates from running. Larger districts also discourage potential candidates who intensely dislike fundraising.

District Marginality   The "safeness" or "competitiveness" of the district—its *marginality*—is often determined more by the distribution of partisan voters within the district than on the presence or absence of an incumbent. For example, between 1978 and 1986, 50 percent of the open seats for the Kentucky General Assembly and 30 percent of the open seats for the Kentucky Senate were uncontested.[32] Most of these were "safe seats" for the Democratic party and the Republicans simply couldn't find anyone to run in a race where a Republican had no chance of getting elected. In cases where one party is decidedly advantaged in a district, the recruitment process is often much different in the majority party compared to the minority party. Whereas many candidates from the majority party may emerge on their own, the minority party will find it difficult to find even one candidate willing to run.

PERSONAL ATTRIBUTES

Campaigning for office takes a personal commitment. Each potential candidate must weigh the personal costs and benefits, and many decide that the costs outweigh the benefits. The general public rarely understands the personal costs involved in running for office, and therefore shows very little appreciation for those who are willing to become candidates. Personal attributes are very important. An individual's previous political experience, personal resources, career goals, sex, race, and ethnicity can have a tremendous impact on his or her success as a candidate.

Previous Political Experience   Prior experience is very helpful in running for office. Candidates with previous experience understand what needs to be done to run a credible campaign. They have greater name recognition among the voters. They have a network of supporters upon whom they can rely for campaign help. The proportion of nonincumbent candidates with prior elective experience varies from state to state.[33]

Personal Resources   Personal resources include the time potential candidates have available to commit to both the campaign and service in the legislature. Campaigning for a state legislative position can be a very draining experience. In a competitive race, candidates may need to campaign eight to ten hours a day for several months. Moreover, serving in the legislature is a full-time job during the time the legislature is in session. Even when not in session, legislators still must devote time to constituent concerns and interim committee meetings. Not many Americans are willing to devote the time necessary to do the job. Personal finances are also a consideration. Most candidates spend at least some of their own money on the campaign. And if the legislature does not provide an adequate salary (and most do not), many potential candidates simply can not make the financial sacrifice to run and serve.

Career Goals   Different people aspire to different sorts of political careers.[34] Some people harbor progressive ambition: a desire to use one political position as a steppingstone to another, higher position. Others have static ambition: a desire to continue in their current elective office for some extended period. Finally, some people have discrete political ambition: brief public service followed by a return to private life. Different career opportunity structures are found in different state legislative settings.[35] This affects not only who runs for state legislative office, but also when they run. In states with strict term limits, for example, it may even change the decision to run at all for the state legislature. Since most of the term limits laws apply to statewide and state legislative offices, but not local offices, the latter may become a more attractive position for those with either static or progressive ambitions.

Sex and Race   Changes in American society have broadened the political and social opportunities available to women and racial minorities. But the pace of such change is not the same everywhere. The political culture in some states, especially southern states, is such that women still have a difficult time getting elected. The same can be said of racial or ethnic minorities in some states.

POLITICAL AMBITION, RATIONAL ACTORS, AND STRATEGIC POLITICIANS

The notion that ambition and politics are intertwined in the American political system goes back at least as far as the *Federalist Papers*, penned over two hundred years ago by Alexander Hamilton, James Madison, and John Jay. The terms "ambition" or "ambitious" show up in at least eight of the *Papers*.[36]

An individual with progressive ambition may find his chances to advance to higher office are so slim that he must give them up, opting to stay in the same office long term (static ambition) or getting out of politics altogether (discrete ambition). Or it may be the case that a candidate initially runs for office thinking she will serve just one or two terms and return to private life, but finds she so enjoys politics that she develops another form of ambition.

It is a common assumption that almost all politicians are progressively ambitious, constantly seeking to move up the hierarchy of political office.[37] This is a key proposition, because it leads us to the related concept of the *strategic politician*.[38] The strategic politician possesses both the desire and understanding of what is necessary to get elected, and astutely assesses political opportunities to further his ambition.[39] In other words, the strategic politician exhibits progressive ambition for office and rationally calculates the chances of winning and the costs involved.

Most of the analysis of strategic politicians focuses on national congressional candidates, and for good reason. A seat in the U.S. House of Representatives or U.S. Senate represents one of the higher rungs on the ladder of political ambition. It is unlikely that very many candidates will successfully reach that rung without prior political experience.[40] Thus, much of the scholarly discussion about strategic ambition centers on the conditions under which "quality candidates" (those with previous political experience) employ this ambition in running for U.S. Congress.

But at the level of state legislative candidacy, these concepts are applied less frequently.[41] There are several reasons for this. First is the American fascination with national institutions, at the expense of state and local institutions. Second is the fact that state legislative office is considered "lower" on the political career ladder, and therefore apparently not worthy of our interest. Third, for many candidates, the state legislature is the first office sought, and the concept of the "strategic politician" therefore seems less appropriate.

It is important to remember that in this book we focus on *nonincumbent* candidates for state legislative office. Most of these candidates do not have well-formulated political career ambitions. Some certainly do, but many of them seem to be activated to run, at least initially, by something other than long-term political ambition. One recent study found that less than one-third of state legislative candidates mentioned "opportunity," in the strategic-politician sense, as a reason for their candidacy.[42] Candidates were far more likely to mention a specific issue that led to their candidacy, and many mentioned citizen duty or party obligations. Our interviews with candidates support this view.

A good example is Mel Lucas, a past mayor of Dauphin Island and former Athletic Director at the University of South Alabama. Lucas characterizes himself as a moderate Republican. His main issue was the need to clean up Mobile Bay, and he challenged the incumbent Republican officeholder in the primary because he felt the incumbent was not sensitive to the environmental issue.

Lucas spent over $20,000 in the primary and was surprised that he got only 25 percent of the primary vote. Asked whether he would have run if he had known he would lose, he said, "Sure. It was something that needed to be done." What was important to him was to raise the issue of the Mobile Bay cleanup.

Or take the case of Bill Wiggins, a Republican challenger for Colorado House Seat 42 in the Denver suburb of Aurora. A commercial real estate broker, Bill had helped develop the Aurora Mall years ago. Recently, some local business leaders had sought a bond issue to finance a new interchange to facilitate access to the mall. Wiggins was the finance director for the bond campaign, and told us, "That's where I locked horns with the incumbent," who was opposed to the bond. Wiggins lost to the incumbent in the general election.

Both the previous examples involved topical challenges to incumbents. This should not be surprising, in many instances challengers are driven by their reaction to the incumbent's stand on an issue. In other cases, challengers are drawn into the decision to run because no one else comes forth. These candidates are often active in local politics and seem to feel some duty to run so that the incumbent doesn't have a "free ride" to reelection. Dan Dean, an attorney and activist in local Democratic politics in Fort Collins, Colorado, was one such candidate. Dean ran against the Republican incumbent "because there was no one else willing to do it." Vic Meyers, a Democratic challenger in a southern Colorado district faced a similar situation. Why would he run against an incumbent in a district that clearly favors Republicans? "My generation doesn't see participation as a duty. We have to get a sense of civic duty back. I do it for my kids—so I can say to them, 'I tried, I was involved.'"

WHO RUNS AND WHY: THE CANDIDATE SURVEY

The most obvious conclusion to draw from the Legislative Candidate Survey is that candidates are still predominantly white and male (see Table 2.2).[43] About 22 percent of the major party respondents were women, and this is reflective of the overall proportion of men-to-women who run for state legislatures nationwide.[44] Well over half the candidates are in their 40s or 50s. As a group, the candidates have achieved a higher education level than is true of the general American population. Over 75 percent of the respondents have attended college, and over 50 percent hold at least a bachelor's degree. Given the level of educational achievement of the candidates, it should come as no surprise that they also report higher-than-average incomes. While fewer than 13 percent have incomes under $30,000, over one-quarter of the respondents reported incomes of $90,000 or more. Well over half of all respondents said their income was at least $50,000. Given the middle- and upper-middle-class nature of the candidates, it is no surprise that they tend to characterize themselves, in terms of political ideology, as moderates (39 percent) or conservatives (34.8 percent).

☑ ADAM CLEMONS, Republican candidate for the Alabama House District 21 open seat, 1998

In many ways, Adam Clemons represents the new generation of southern politicos. He is bright, well mannered, and friendly. He is clearly ambitious, and sees the Republican party as the party of the future in the South. Clemons is very young, just twenty-one years old, but has already worked on several campaigns in the past—as a Democrat. In fact, as a seventeen-year-old he worked on the 1994 campaign of State Representative Randy Hinshaw, who is vacating this seat to run for the state senate.

Clemons, a student at Auburn University, had previously toyed with the idea of competing against Hinshaw for the house seat. When Hinshaw decided to run for the senate, Clemons jumped in. He took a year off from college and came home to Huntsville to run for the open house seat.

Soon after the 1994 election, Clemons had switched to the Republican party. In fact, he was chosen to be president of the Auburn University College Republicans in 1996, and later became chairman of the College Republican Federation of Alabama (a coalition of Republican students from all the college campuses in Alabama). That experience put him in contact with influential people in the GOP state organization, since the presidents of the student GOP organizations are ex-officio members of the state party steering committee.

His previous work on campaigns means he knows the district very well, and he is working the district hard. He has thought out his campaign strategy carefully. Even though the district has traditionally been a Democratic stronghold, the Republicans are making in-roads and Clemons is convinced that the time is right for a GOP candidate to win the district. His campaign brochures are very professional. He is walking a good part of the district, has sent out five direct mailings, and hopes to hire a consulting firm from Birmingham to help with media buys, "if I get enough money." The party provided some funding, and eventually he managed to collect over $40,000 in campaign contributions—a hefty sum for a first-time candidate.

Win or lose, it is unlikely that this will be the last election in which we hear from Adam Clemons. Even at his young age, he has a pleasant and mature personal style, and is comfortable in the public role of the campaign. He already exhibits the characteristics political scientists have in mind when they speak of the "strategic politician."

Adam Clemons lost the election in a surprising Democratic resurgence in Alabama. He returned to Auburn University to finish his degree. While back at Auburn, he started his own company developing internet web sites, and has been working with the state GOP to build web sites for each of the county Republican party organizations.

This is Adam B. Clemons...

When it comes to fighting for our future, no other candidate can compare to Adam B. Clemons. Born in Huntsville, he went to school and lives in the Riverton area. He is the son of a county school teacher and former Huntsville City firefighter.

At the young age of 9, he became interested in politics and has pursued his goals ever since.

He's been involved with his church. He's volunteered in his community. He's preparing to become a History Teacher.

He's been given awards. He's created a high school scholarship. He's served on state and national boards. He's been a leader and a fighter.

But this campaign is not about what Adam has accomplished. It's about changing Alabama. It's about being our voice in the 21st Century.

Labels have never fit Adam. In Montgomery, the only label he will have is that of State Representative.

If standing up for us means fighting the PACs or going against the governor, then so be it. He'll represent our concerns - not the liberal trial lawyers or any special interest group.

We need someone like that working for us. We need someone who will be an independent thinker, not a partisan politician. We need Adam B. Clemons

The Adam Clemons material is reprinted with the permission of Adam Clemons.

TABLE 2.2   BACKGROUND CHARACTERISTICS
OF MAJOR PARTY CANDIDATE RESPONDENTS

Party Affiliation (N = 538)	Republican (N = 265)	49.3%
	Democrat (N = 273)	50.7
Ideology (N = 534)	Very Conservative	9.7%
	Conservative	34.8
	Moderate	39.0
	Liberal	14.4
	Very Liberal	2.1
Office Sought (N = 538)	Lower Chamber (N = 479)	77.3%
	State Senate (N = 130)	22.7
Gender (N = 536)	Male	78.4%
	Female	21.6
Race/Ethnicity (N = 530)	African-American	4.7%
	Caucasian	92.6
	Hispanic	1.1
	Other	1.5
Education (N = 538)	Less than H.S.	5.9%
	H.S. graduate	16.7
	Some college	26.4
	College grad.	41.3
	Post-graduate	9.7
Annual Income (N = 389)*	Under $30,000	12.3%
	$30K–$49,999	24.2
	$50K–$69,999	18.8
	$70K–$89,999	17.5
	$90K–$119,999	11.8
	Over $120,000	15.4
Age (N = 538)	Under 30	5.0%
	30–39	17.8
	40–49	29.2
	50–59	29.7
	60–69	15.4
	over 70	2.8
Occupation (N = 520)	Business employee	16.0%
	Retired	15.4
	Business owner	13.7
	Attorney	10.4
	Educator	8.7
	Government employee	5.6
	Real estate/insurance	4.4
	Medical employee	3.5
	Farmer/rancher	3.5
	Other	18.8
Marital status (N = 531)	Never married	11.4%
	Married	74.9
	Divorced/separated	11.4
	Widowed	2.3

TABLE 2.2, CONT.

Children living at home?	No	52.1%
(N = 537)	Yes	47.9
How long have you lived in	Less than 2 years	3.6%
the community? (N = 535)	3–5 years	9.3
	6–10 years	11.4
	More than 10 years	75.7

*N is smaller here because the question was not asked in Washington or Colorado.

Source: Survey of Nonincumbent State Legislative Candidates (hereafter referred to as The Legislative Candidate Survey), conducted in 1997 and 1998 by Gary F. Moncrief and Peverill Squire.

The occupational background of nonincumbent legislative candidates is different than what the general public probably imagines. For example, only about 10 percent of the candidates are attorneys.[45] Over the years, there has been a decline in the number of attorneys willing to run because many state legislatures today have longer sessions than in the past, and it has become more difficult to balance one's profession with the time necessary to serve in the legislature.

Almost three out of ten candidates have a business background (16 percent as business employees, 13.7 percent as business owners). Surprisingly, the second-largest occupational group is "retired" (15.4 percent). This, in fact, reflects the nature of state legislative life. Unlike the U.S. Congress, most state legislatures meet for only a few (usually three to five) months each year and the legislative salary is usually commensurate with the time commitment. In other words, it requires a substantial time investment but it is not a full-time occupation and does not pay a full-time salary. Retirees are better able to accommodate the time commitment and salary limitations than are people with full-time jobs. This dynamic is not true everywhere, of course. Serving in the Michigan legislature, for example, basically requires a full-time commitment and pays a full-time salary.

This time commitment is also reflected in the family situation of most candidates. While the overwhelming majority (74.9 percent) of the respondents are married, most (52.1 percent) of the candidates do not have children living at home. Finally, candidates are deeply rooted in their communities. More than three out of four of the respondents have lived in the community for at least ten years: Only 3.6 percent are relative newcomers.

THE POLITICAL BACKGROUNDS OF THE CANDIDATES

How politically experienced are the nonincumbent candidates? Most are novices; only 23 percent have run for the state legislature before. As we might expect, relatively few have held previous political office (see Table 2.3). Less

TABLE 2.3   POLITICAL EXPERIENCE OF MAJOR PARTY CANDIDATES

Run for legislature before? (N = 465)*	No	76.3%
	Lost primary	7.1
	Won primary	16.6
Currently hold elective office (N = 537)	No	75.2%
	Yes	24.8
Currently hold appointive office (N = 538)	No	90.3%
	Yes	9.7
Served on legislative staff (N = 499)*	No	91.2%
	State legislative staff	4.5
	Congressional staff	3.0
	Both	1.3
Held political party position (N = 536)	None	39.9%
	Local	51.1
	State/national	16.2
	Convention delegate	33.0

*N is lower because this question did not appear on the New Jersey survey.
Note: Percentages exceed 100 percent in "Held political party position" because multiple responses are possible.
Source: Legislative Candidate Survey

than one out of four held elective office at the time he became a candidate for the state legislature. However, this aggregate figure masks rather substantial state-to-state variation. While few candidates in Alabama (10.1 percent) had elective experience, a much higher percentage of candidates in term-limited states such as Colorado (28.1 percent) and Maine (26.5 percent) held elective office. Most are local offices such as city council, school board, or county commission seats. A few, however, were members of the lower chamber of the state legislature now running for a senate seat. This is an important point in regard to states with state legislative term limits. Because term limits create more open seats, "strategic politicians" from the local level appear to be more likely to run for a legislative seat.

Another interesting case is New Jersey. While not a state with legislative term limits, New Jersey is unique in that legislators are permitted to hold local office concurrently; in other words, one does not have to give up one's local office if elected to the state legislature. Consequently, a substantial number of locally elected officials run for the legislature.[46]

There is a clear relationship between open-seat candidates and political experience (see Table 2.4). Of those candidates challenging an incumbent from their own party in the primary election, only 15.4 percent held elective office. A somewhat higher percentage (20.7 percent) of the candidates who challenged an incumbent from the other party in the general election were officeholders. But when there is no incumbent in the race (the seat is open), 31.2 percent of the candidates had held elective office.[47]

TABLE 2.4   ELECTIVE OFFICE EXPERIENCE
AND TYPE OF CANDIDACY (MAJOR PARTY CANDIDATES)

CANDIDATE STATUS	CURRENTLY HOLDING ELECTIVE OFFICE
Primary Challenger	15.4%
General Challenger	20.7
Open Seat	31.2

Note: N = 534
Source: The Legislative Candidate Survey

To put this another way, a majority (54.9 percent) of those candidates currently holding elective office ran as open-seat contestants rather than as challengers to an incumbent (see Table 2.5). In other words, they meet the definition of the "strategic politician" pursuing "progressive ambition." On the other hand, almost 60 percent of the candidates *without* electoral experience ran as challengers.

Sixty percent of candidates have experience working on a campaign, serving in a party position such as precinct captain or on a county central committee, or as a delegate to a state or national party convention. Over half reported that they had served at the local party level, usually as a local precinct committeeman or committeewoman, or as District or County Party Chair. A good example is Diana Holland, an unsuccessful candidate for an open seat in Colorado. A long-time resident of the area, she had served as Arapahoe County Democratic Party Chair between 1991 and 1995, and in that capacity she "did a lot of candidate recruitment." She was Democratic Chair for House District 38 when she decided to run in 1998.

Even if they have not held an official position with their party, many of the candidates have experience working on campaigns at the national, state, and local level (see Table 2.6). They are especially likely to have been active locally; over 70 percent say they have been active or very active in local campaigns or state legislative races.

TABLE 2.5   THE RELATIONSHIP BETWEEN ELECTIVE EXPERIENCE
AND TYPE OF CANDIDACY (MAJOR PARTY CANDIDATES)

CURRENTLY HOLD ELECTIVE OFFICE?	CHALLENGER	OPEN SEAT
No (N = 401)	59.9%	40.1%
Yes (N = 133)	45.1	54.9

Note: Chi-square = 8.81; df = 1; p<.01
Source: Legislative Candidate Survey

TABLE 2.6   PREVIOUS WORK ON POLITICAL CAMPAIGNS (MAJOR PARTY CANDIDATES)

TYPE OF CAMPAIGN	NOT ACTIVE	ACTIVE	VERY ACTIVE
Federal (N = 487)	37.1%	40.6%	22.2%
Statewide (N = 483)	34.1	40.7	25.0
Local (N = 497)	26.6	33.0	40.4
State Legislative (N = 497)	28.5	38.7	32.7

Source: Legislative Candidate Survey

How, then, do we summarize these tables on the backgrounds of nonincumbent candidates? As a group, they are predominantly well educated, in their 40s or 50s, married, and male. Many of them have experience in the business world. There are many fewer attorneys and more retirees than we might expect.

While many of the candidates have been active in their local party organizations, few have held public office; indeed, relatively few of them have ever run for office before. For many, while they have worked on campaigns for others, this is the first time they crossed that threshold from political activism to political candidacy. It marks a major event in their lives. For most of these people, then, their campaign for state legislature is quite a new learning experience.

Notably, candidates with elective experience are far more likely to wait for an open seat than to challenge an incumbent. These people exhibit the characteristics of the "strategic politician" so pervasive in studies of the U.S. Congress. Nonetheless—and this is the essential point—most of the nonincumbent candidates at the state legislative level can not be characterized as strategic politicians. They are running for public office for the first time, without much thought to a long-term political career. They are running because they are actively involved in community affairs and because political office seems to them an extension of that community involvement.

THE DECISION TO RUN

When did these candidates decide to run for office? Over half of the candidates made their decision within five months of the primary (see Table 2.7). There are some interesting variations from state to state, however. For example, a substantial proportion of the respondents from Iowa (44.2 percent) and Virginia (46.4 percent) reported making the decision within two months of the primary. In Colorado, only 17 percent made the same claim. These differences are based, in part, on the variation in state electoral laws. Some states have earlier deadlines for filing candidacy petitions, for example. And in Colorado, because the district nominating caucuses are held prior to the primary election, serious candidates can not wait until the last month or so to decide on their candidacy.

TABLE 2.7   "WHEN DID YOU PERSONALLY MAKE THE DECISION
TO BECOME A CANDIDATE IN THIS RACE?"

HOW MANY MONTHS BEFORE THE PRIMARY?	N = 537
Within 2 months	27.8%
3–5 months	28.9
6–12 months	23.5
More than a year	19.8

Source: The Legislative Candidate Survey

Almost 20 percent of the candidates made the decision to run more than a year before the primary election, indicating a long-term commitment on their part. The figures are especially high in Michigan, Colorado, and Maine—all states with term limits.[48] The existence of term limits means that potential candidates know when an incumbent will be forced out and the seat will become open, and therefore potential candidates can begin to plan accordingly.

Most candidates had been entertaining the idea of running for awhile. Only about 21 percent said they had not seriously thought about running until someone else suggested they do so (see Table 2.8). We can characterize this group as the *persuaded*. A good example is Lynda Straub of Alabama; it had simply never occurred to her to run for office until some influential people in her community approached her about the possibility (see her candidate profile, in Chapter 5).

At the other end of the spectrum are the pure *self-starters*, who reported "it was entirely my idea to run."[49] Laura Ruderman is such a person. She came to the Seattle area from the East Coast a mere four years before she decided to run. While she had been involved since high school in a grassroots lobbying group whose aim was to help relieve hunger and poverty, she had never held any elective office or even been very active in local party politics. But at the age of twenty-seven, she decided to challenge a one-term incumbent in a suburban district near Seattle. In so doing, she became one of the youngest candidates to run for the Washington House of Representatives in 1998. She ran an exhausting campaign for six months, working "fifteen hours a day, seven days a week." Her determination and energy paid off; she defeated the incumbent in the general election.

Clearly, there are more self-starters (32.1 percent) than those who can be called *persuaded*, although perhaps the self-starters are not as large a group as we might expect, given all the talk in the United States about "ambitious politicians" and "candidate-centered" elections. The largest group (46.6 percent) is what we will call the *encouraged*. These people had been mulling over the notion of running, but had not yet decided what to do, when someone else encouraged them to run.

TABLE 2.8   "WHOSE IDEA WAS IT TO RUN FOR LEGISLATURE?"

It was entirely my idea	32.1%
I had already thought about it when someone else encouraged me to run	46.6
I had not seriously thought about it until someone else suggested it	21.3

Note: N = 464. This question was asked in different form in New Jersey and is therefore not directly compara-
ble. New Jersey respondents are excluded from the table.
Source: Legislative Candidate Survey

PATTERNS OF COMMUNICATION AND THE CANDIDACY

Only about one-third of the candidates characterize themselves as truly "self-
starters." The rest of the candidates required some encouragement or push
before they committed to running. So whom did they talk with? (See Table 2.9)

It comes as no surprise that "family and friends have the greatest influence over the decision to run for office."[50] After all, running for office requires
not only a commitment from the candidate, but it has important consequences
for other family members as well. The discussion with the family about potential candidacy is a quite different sort of dialogue than talks with other
groups. For one thing, the family members are directly affected by the candidacy in ways other groups are not. Other group discussions are more likely
to be especially encouraging of the potential candidate, because (with the possible exception of business partners) there is no cost to these other groups;
they really have nothing to lose by encouraging the potential candidate to
run. There are, however, costs to other family members. One individual told
us that her candidacy meant her two teenage sons had to do all the grocery

TABLE 2.9   "BEFORE YOU ANNOUNCED YOUR CANDIDACY, DID YOU DISCUSS
THE MATTER WITH ANY OF THE FOLLOWING PEOPLE OR GROUPS?"

Family	92.9%
Officials in the local party	69.3
Local elected officials	51.9
Leaders in the state legislature	51.9
Officials in the state party	50.3
Co-workers/business partners	49.4
Friends/acquaintances in my neighborhood	36.1
Friends/acquaintances in a service organization	33.2
Friends/acquaintances from church	28.7
Members of an interest group or association	19.4
Other	9.3

Note: N = 535
Source: Legislative Candidate Survey

shopping and learn to cook for themselves because she was out campaigning each afternoon and evening. Another lamented the fact that he was missing all of his kid's soccer and football games. Another, who had run for office once before, told us his wife was very upset with him when the local party leaders asked him to run again and he agreed to be the candidate.

After the family, the groups most likely to be consulted are party leaders. Almost 70 percent of the candidates said they discussed their possible candidacy with local party officials; about half said they talked with state party officials, legislative leaders, and locally-elected officials. In other words, even in the American world of candidate-centered campaigns and elections, parties are still an important part of the candidacy network. For one thing, potential candidates want to know who else is thinking about running. Few candidates want to undertake both a tough primary campaign *and* a general election race. It is quite rational for an individual to seek information from the party about other potential candidates. Moreover, the potential candidate wants to know what (if any) support they can expect to receive from the party.

About half of the candidates discussed their potential candidacy with co-workers or business partners. In the case of business partners, the potential impact of the campaign may have consequences in at least two ways. First, it may mean others in the business must pick up some of the workload since the candidate will be on the campaign trail. Second, some businesses—especially smaller businesses—may fear that the appearance of partisanship will drive some customers away.

Interest groups, associates in service organizations like the Kiwanis or Junior League, and friends from church or the neighborhood were less likely to be consulted.

Primary challengers were consistently less likely to discuss the situation with party officials than were general election challengers or open seat contestants (see Table 2.10 on page 42). This makes sense, of course. A primary challenge is an internecine conflict; it is essentially an electoral attack on a fellow party-member—and an incumbent to boot. It is highly unlikely that such challenges will be looked upon favorably by the party elite. But there is more to the pattern than this. While primary challengers are consistently less likely to discuss their potential candidacy with party officials, they are consistently *more* likely to discuss it with nonparty contacts. Clearly, primary challengers see themselves as party outsiders, and they seek advice and encouragement from individuals and groups outside the party organization.

Most candidates talked to more than one group about their potential candidacy. Candidates reported discussing their potential candidacy with an average of almost five different types of groups (see Table 2.11 on page 42).[51] This includes the family—a group with which almost all candidates said they discussed the candidacy issue. So the average number of groups *outside the family* is about four. Across candidate status, there is very little difference in the average number of groups contacted.

TABLE 2.10   Discussions with Others, by Candidate Status
(Percent of Respondents Who Say They Discussed Their Potential
Candidacy with Party and Nonparty Groups)

	Primary Challenger (N = 39)	General Challenger (N = 262)	Open Seat (N = 234)
Party Contacts			
Local Party Officials	53.8%	77.9%	62.2%
State Party Officials	23.1	58.4	45.9
Local Elected Officials	46.2	47.3	57.7
Legislative Leaders	33.3	53.8	53.4
Nonparty Contacts			
Church Members	43.6%	29.5%	24.4%
Neighbors	56.4	38.3	29.9
Interest Groups	28.2	18.0	19.7
Co-workers	59.0	49.0	47.4
Service Organizations	38.5	31.5	33.8

Source: Legislative Candidate Survey

TABLE 2.11   Average Number of Groups/Individuals with Whom
Candidate Discussed Candidacy

	Avg. Number of Contacts	Standard Deviation
Candidate Status		
General challenger (N = 260)	5.04	2.41
Primary challenger (N = 39)	4.85	2.35
Open seat (N = 232)	4.79	2.18
Timing of Decision		
Within 2 months (N = 148)	4.48	2.30
3–5 months (N = 152)	4.74	2.05
6–12 months (N = 126)	5.45	2.19
More than a year (N = 105)	5.16	2.63
*Whose Idea to Run?**		
Self-starters (N = 150)	4.16	2.34
Encouraged (N = 216)	5.42	2.26
Persuaded (N = 98)	5.33	2.04
Totals (N = 531)	4.91	2.30

*p<.01 between self-starters and encouraged and between self-starters and persuaded. New Jersey data are not included, due to a difference in question format.
Source: Legislative Candidate Survey

There is a significant difference, however, based on *when* the candidate decided to run. Not surprisingly, those who entered the race within two months of the primary consulted fewer groups than those who entered the race at least six months before the primary. As we would expect, self-starters (mean = 4.16 contacts) consulted fewer groups than those who had to be encouraged (mean = 5.42) or persuaded (mean = 5.33) to run. Again, the family is one of the groups included in these figures.

PATTERNS OF RECRUITMENT AND THE CANDIDACY

Communication is a two-way street. Sometimes the discussions are initiated by the political party, or an interest group or someone else. In other words, agents of political recruitment may seek out potential candidates and try to persuade them to run.

Party officials are the most likely sources of recruitment contact (see Table 2.12). Particularly active in this regard are local party officials: 46.1 percent of all major party candidates said that they had been approached and encouraged to run by officials from the local party. For state legislative races, it is logical that this would be the most common party contact. Moreover, about a third of the candidates said they received recruitment contacts from elected officials, state legislative leaders, or state party officials.

It is something of a surprise that the candidates did not report *more* recruitment contacts by various party elements. More than half said they had not been recruited by the local political party organization. State party officials contacted even fewer of the candidates. A small percentage of candidates said that someone from an interest group or association approached them about running.

TABLE 2.12   "BEFORE YOU ANNOUNCED YOUR CANDIDACY, WERE YOU
APPROACHED AND ENCOURAGED TO RUN FOR OFFICE BY ANY OF THE FOLLOWING?"
(PERCENT ANSWERING "YES")

Officials in the local party	46.1%
Local elected officials	33.5
Leaders in the state legislature	33.3
Officials in the state party	32.9
Family members	32.7
Friends/acquaintances in my neighborhood	22.7
Co-workers/business partners	19.0
Friends/acquaintances in a service organization	17.7
Members of an interest group/association	13.6
Friends/acquaintances from church	12.1
Other	7.8

Note: $N = 535$
Source: Legislative Candidate Survey

The local party more actively recruits candidates to challenge the opposition party's incumbents (see Table 2.13). General election challengers are more likely (55.7 percent) to report recruitment contact with local party officials than are primary challengers (28.2 percent) or open seat contestants (38.5 percent). The local party sees one of its main functions as finding people to run against the other party's incumbents. Finding candidates for open seat contests is not usually a problem; numerous candidates make the decision to enter an open seat race without having been recruited by the party. Nor is the party likely to recruit candidates to run against its own incumbents. Less than 13 percent of the primary challengers were contacted by legislative leaders, while over one-third of both general election challengers and open seat contestants were contacted. Primary challengers display the communication patterns of outsiders—in terms of whom they discussed their candidacy with and who actively recruited them.

In terms of average number of recruitment contacts, there is no meaningful difference by candidate status (see Table 2.14). The most dramatic difference in reported recruitment contacts, however, is between self-starters and those who were encouraged or persuaded to run. Just as we would expect, self-starters were significantly less likely to report recruitment contacts.

There is a significant difference in party recruitment contacts between self-starters and others. It is also worth noting that some candidates reported recruitment contacts from several party organizations (state party, local party, elected officials). Although these party organizations often work independently of one another, it is clear that in some cases, when there is a particularly attractive potential candidate available, they will use the "full-court press" technique to persuade the individual to run.

TABLE 2.13   RECRUITMENT PATTERNS, BY CANDIDATE STATUS (PERCENT OF RESPONDENTS WHO SAY THEY WERE APPROACHED BY VARIOUS PARTY AND NON-PARTY GROUPS)

	PRIMARY CHALLENGER (N = 39)	GENERAL CHALLENGER (N = 262)	OPEN SEAT (N = 234)
PARTY CONTACTS			
Local Party Officials	28.2%	55.7%	38.5%
State Party Officials	20.5	36.3	31.2
Local Elected Officials	33.3	30.5	36.3
Legislative Leaders	12.8	35.5	34.6
NONPARTY CONTACTS			
Church Members	17.9%	12.2%	10.7%
Neighbors	46.2	21.8	20.1
Interest groups	15.4	12.6	14.5
Co-workers	25.6	18.3	18.8
Service Organizations	15.4	19.1	16.7

Source: Legislative Candidate Survey

TABLE 2.14   AVERAGE NUMBER OF RECRUITMENT CONTACTS

	AVG. NUMBER OF RECRUITMENT CONTACTS (S.D.)	AVG. NUMBER OF PARTY RECRUITMENT CONTACTS (S.D.)
*CANDIDATE STATUS**		
General challenger (*N* = 262)	2.50 (2.18)	1.58 (1.35)
Primary challenger (*N* = 39)	2.25 (2.12)	0.95 (1.31)
Open seat (*N* = 234)	2.29 (1.94)	1.40 (1.31)
TIMING OF DECISION		
Within 2 months (*N* = 149)	2.06 (2.00)	1.29 (1.30)
3–5 months (*N* = 155)	2.39 (2.09)	1.52 (1.26)
6–12 months (*N* = 127)	2.73 (2.08)	1.69 (1.38)
More than a year (*N* = 105)	2.44 (2.34)	1.35 (1.43)
*WHOSE IDEA TO RUN***		
Self-starters (*N* = 150)	1.58 (1.95)	0.78 (1.21)
Encouraged (*N* = 217)	3.36 (2.32)	1.78 (1.31)
Persuaded (*N* = 99)	3.02 (2.09)	1.74 (1.27)
Totals (*N* = 535)		

*statistically significant (p<.01) for party contacts but not for total contacts
**statistically significant (p<.01) for both party contacts and total contacts
New Jersey data are not included in the question about "Whose Idea to Run."
Source: Legislative Candidate Survey

CONCLUSION

Earlier we noted some of the costs and benefits of running for the state legislature. Each potential candidate must weigh these costs and benefits for herself or himself, individually. In the end, it is an intensely personal decision. The collective result of these individual decisions has an important impact on state legislative races in the United States.

A voter's task is largely limited to choosing between those candidates who make the decision to run. Most of those who run are a decidedly middle-class group with deep roots in their community. They are often middle-aged and, surprisingly, likely to be "empty-nesters." They are more likely to be business owners, business employees, or retirees than attorneys. They tend to be fairly active in local politics, but comparatively few of them have ever run for office before. Their activism has been confined to volunteer work on other campaigns, or to local party office such as precinct captain. As a group, they do not come close to meeting the definition of "professional politician." However, those candidates who do have prior office-holding experience are more likely to behave strategically, waiting for an open seat before they run for the legislature.

Some rather distinct patterns emerge when we look at candidate status. In particular, primary election challengers are a different lot than general election challengers or open seat contestants. They talk to fewer people about their potential candidacy and are rarely recruited by the political party.

For most of the candidates, the decision to run was not made in a vacuum. They discussed the situation with a number of different groups. In particular, family members were part of the discussion. The most common recruitment agents were political party or elected officials. Yet fewer than half of the candidates said they were approached and encouraged to run by the local party, and fewer still reported such contacts from the state party or other party officials. What are the conditions under which the political party actively recruits candidates? What does the party look for in a candidate? These and related questions are addressed in the next chapter.

NOTES

1. Alan Ehrenhalt, *The United States of Ambition* (New York: Random House, 1991), 149.
2. Richard Tobin and Edward Keynes, "Institutional Differences in the Recruitment Process: A Four State Study," *American Journal of Political Science* 19 (1975): 671.
3. There are no comprehensive data on legislative endorsement results. We do know, however, that in recent years in gubernatorial primaries the endorsed candidate has won about 75 percent of the time. It is likely that, in legislative primaries, endorsed candidates are even more successful. For further discussion of the endorsement process, see Malcolm E. Jewell and Sarah M. Morehouse, "State Political Party Endorsements: Continuity and Change" (Paper presented at the Annual Meeting of the Midwest Political Science Association, Chicago, April 1999).
4. This index is from Peverill Squire, "Uncontested Seats in State Legislative Elections," *Legislative Studies Quarterly* 25 (2000): 131–146, and was calculated using recent data on regular session legislative compensation, the mean number of legislative days in regular session, and the number of staff members in each state legislature. The data in each category for each state were compared to that for the U.S. Congress for the same time period. In essence, the final score for each state can be interpreted as revealing how closely that state legislature mirrors the U.S. Congress in terms of professionalization. In this sense, professionalization refers to the commitment of resources and time to the task of legislation. The concept should not be construed to suggest that part-time, "citizen" legislators do not behave in a competent, professional manner.
5. Morris Fiorina, *Divided Government*, 2nd ed. (Boston: Allyn & Bacon, Inc., 1996), 48.
6. Daniel Shea, *Transforming Democracy: Legislative Campaign Committees and Political Parties* (Albany: State University of New York Press, 1995).
7. Ehrenhalt, *The United State of Ambition*; and Fiorina, *Divided Government*.

8. Peverill Squire, "Career Opportunities and Membership Stability in Legislatures," *Legislative Studies Quarterly* 13 (1988): 65–81.

9. Gary F. Moncrief, "Candidate Spending in State Legislative Races," in *Campaign Finance in State Legislative Elections*, ed. Joel A. Thompson and Gary F. Moncrief (Washington, D.C.: CQ Press, 1998).

10. Sandy Maisel and Elizabeth Ivry, "If You Don't Like Our Politics, Wait A Minute: Party Politics in Maine at the End of the Twentieth Century," *Polity*, Special supplement (1997), 35.

11. It should be noted that the Colorado law was struck down in August 1999 in U.S. District Court. As of this writing, the case is on appeal.

12. Nor is the evidence from other states particularly consistent. For example, both Minnesota and Wisconsin offer a measure of public funding for state legislative races if candidates agree to limit their overall campaign spending. One study of the Minnesota system concludes that public funding has made for more competitive elections. On the other hand, a study of the Wisconsin law finds that it has not made elections more competitive. See Patrick Donnay and Graham Ramsden, "Public Financing of Legislative Elections: Lessons from Minnesota," *Legislative Studies Quarterly* 20 (1995): 351–364; and Kenneth Mayer and John M. Wood, "The Impact of Public Financing on Electoral Competitiveness: Evidence From Wisconsin, 1964–1990," *Legislative Studies Quarterly* 20 (1995): 69–88.

13. Albert Nelson, *The Emerging Influentials in State Legislatures: Women, Blacks and Hispanics* (New York: Praeger, 1991).

14. Tom Loftus, *The Art of Legislative Politics* (Washington, D.C.: CQ Press, 1991), 36.

15. This quote first appeared in Gary F. Moncrief, Peverill Squire, and Karl Kurtz, "Gateways to the Statehouse" (Paper presented at the 1998 Annual Meeting of the American Political Science Association, Boston, Mass.). We want to acknowledge Karl Kurtz for his help in interviewing state legislative leaders for that paper.

16. Daniel Elazar, *American Federalism: A View from the States*, 3rd ed. (New York: Harper & Row, 1984).

17. Nelson, *The Emerging Influentials in State Legislatures*; and Susan Vandenbosch, "Evidence for an Inverse Relationship Between the Percentage of Women State Legislators and the Percentage of Christian Church Adherents in the States" (Paper presented at the 1995 Annual Meeting of the Southern Political Science Association, Tampa, Fla.).

18. See, for example, Krista Jenkins and Susan Carroll, "The Effect of Term Limits on the Representation of Women: An Analysis of Evidence from the 1998 Elections," *Social Science Quarterly*, Forthcoming, 2000.

19. Paul Herrnson, *Congressional Elections: Campaigning at Home and in Washington*, 2nd ed. (Washington, D.C.: CQ Press, 1998), 59.

20. Moncrief and Thompson, "Candidate Spending in State Legislative Races," 54.

21. Jeffrey M. Cummins and Nathan D. Woods, "Campaign Spending and Its Effects in the 1996 California Legislative Elections" (Paper presented at the Annual Meeting of the Western Political Science Association, Seattle, Wash., March 1999).

22. David Breaux and Malcolm E. Jewell, "Winning Big: The Incumbency Advantage in State Legislative Races," in *Changing Patterns in State Legislative Careers*, ed. Gary F. Moncrief and Joel A. Thompson (Ann Arbor: University of Michigan Press, 1992), 93–94.

23. Breaux and Jewell, "Winning Big: The Incumbency Advantage," 103.

24. Wayne Francis, "House to Senate Career Movement in the U.S. States: The Significance of Selectivity," *Legislative Studies Quarterly* 18 (1993): 309–320.

25. James L. Gibson, John Frendreis, and Laura Vertz, "Party Dynamics in the 1980s: Change in the County Party Organizations' Strength, 1980–84," *American Journal of Political Science* 33 (1989): 67–90. Also see John Frendreis, Alan Gitelson, Gregory Fleming, and Anne Layzell, "Local Parties and Legislative Races in 1992 and 1994," in *The State of the Parties*, 2nd ed., ed. John Green and Daniel M. Shea (Lanham, Md.: Rowman and Littlefield, 1996).

26. Lester Seligman, Michael King, Chong Lim Kim, and Roland Smith, *Patterns of Recruitment: A State Chooses Its Lawmakers* (Chicago: Rand McNally, 1974), 76.

27. Ehrenhalt, *The United States of Ambition*.

28. John Heilprin, "Mormons Urged to Seek Political Office," *Salt Lake City Tribune* 3 February 1998.

29. See, for example, Gary Cox and Scott Morgenstern, "The Incumbency Advantage in Multimember Districts: Evidence From the States," *Legislative Studies Quarterly* 20 (1995): 329–349.

30. Bernard Grofman and Lisa Handley, "Black Representation: Making Sense of Electoral Geography at Different Levels of Government," *Legislative Studies Quarterly* 14 (1989): 265–279.

31. Robert Hogan and Keith Hamm, "Variations in District-Level Campaign Spending in State Legislatures," in *Campaign Finance in State Legislative Elections*, ed. Joel A. Thompson and Gary F. Moncrief (Washington, D.C.: CQ Press, 1998).

32. Breaux and Jewell, "Winning Big: The Incumbency Advantage."

33. Emily Van Dunk, "Challenger Quality in State Legislative Elections," *Political Research Quarterly* 50 (1997): 793–807.

34. Joseph Schlesinger, *Ambition and Politics* (Chicago: Rand McNally, 1966).

35. Squire, "Career Opportunities and Membership Stability in Legislatures," 67.

36. Hamilton appears to have been particularly cognizant of ambition as a component of human nature. He makes reference to it in at least *Papers*: #6, #17, #22, #27, #30, #72, and #75. Madison mentions it in #51.

37. One of the best expressions of this premise is David Rohde, "Risk-Bearing and Progressive Ambition: The Case of Members of the United States House of Representatives," *American Journal of Political Science* 23 (1978): 1–26.

38. See Gary Jacobson and Samuel Kernell, *Strategy and Choice in Congressional Elections* (New Haven: Yale University Press, 1981).

39. Paul Herrnson, *Congressional Elections: Campaigning at Home and in Washington*, 30.

40. It is fair to note, however, that around 25 percent of the members of Congress have not held prior political office. See David Canon, *Actors, Athletes and Astronauts: Political Amateurs in the United States* (Chicago: University of Chicago Press, 1990).

41. This is not to say they are never applied. Two good examples of the use of such concepts at the level of state legislative research are: Anita Pritchard, "Strategic Considerations in the Decision to Challenge a State Legislative Incumbent," *Legislative Studies Quarterly* 17 (1992): 381–394; and Van Dunk, "Challenger Quality in State Legislative Elections," 793–807.

42. John Frendreis, Alan Gitelson, Shannon Jenkins, and Douglas Roscoe, "Candidate Emergence in State Politics" (Paper presented at the Annual Meeting of the Western Political Science Association, Seattle, Wash., March 1999), 14, 32.

43. The general background characteristics are shown in Table 2.2. The tables in this chapter report data only from major party candidates (Democrats and Republicans), since the overwhelming majority of candidates in state legislatures run under one of these two party banners. The major party survey respondents are almost evenly split between Republicans and Democrats (49.3 percent and 50.7 percent, respectively). In our research, we also surveyed a group of candidates running as members of other parties (known collectively in the United States as "third party" or "minor party" candidates). These included candidates from parties as diverse as the Libertarian, Taxpayer's Union, Conservative, Socialist, and Green parties. Since third party nominees represent only a small portion of the candidacies in the United States, we discuss them separately, in Chapter 5.

While our respondent group generally reflects the true population of candidates, it should be noted that our sample does underrepresent minority groups slightly. We think this is due to the fact that we are excluding incumbent legislators from our study. Since many minorities are elected from safe-seat districts, there are few minority challengers to incumbents. Aside from this drawback, the sample appears to be a fairly accurate reflection of the population of all nonincumbent legislative candidates.

44. The Center for American Women and Politics, Eagleton Institute, Rutgers University, reports that 24.9 percent of all nonincumbent state legislative candidates in 1998 were women. See CAWP Fact Sheet: Women Candidates For State Legislatures, Election Results 1988, 1992, 1994, 1996 & 1998.

45. Although attorneys only comprise perhaps 10 percent of all candidates, the proportion of elected state legislators who are attorneys is somewhat higher: 16.5 percent according to a 1993 survey conducted by the National Conference of State Legislatures. The discrepancy between the proportion of *candidates* who are lawyers and the proportion of *legislators* who are attorneys is probably explained by the fact that lawyers are often especially good candidates since they have superior verbal skills and tend to think strategically.

46. It is also evident from Table 2.3 that few of the candidates have held legislative staff positions or appointed political office. Less than 10 percent of the respondents had served in either type of position. There is, however, some variation in this regard by state. For example, fewer than 7 percent of the Alabama and Iowa candidates had held appointive office, while 14 percent of the candidates in Colorado and New Jersey held such office.

47. This is a statistically significant difference: chi-square = 9.402, df = 2, p<.01.

48. The percentage of respondents who said they decided to run at least twelve months prior to the primary election are: Michigan 33.3 percent; Colorado 28.1 percent; Maine 20.5 percent; Washington 19.2 percent; Alabama 16.7 percent; New Jersey 14.3 percent; Virginia 14.3 percent; and Iowa 13.0 percent. The total number of respondents for each state, respectively, is 51, 64, 83, 73, 90, 70, 28, 77. We must be cautious about analyzing state-by-state data because of the smaller number of cases per state, but these figures do suggest that term limits have an effect on the timing of the decision to run. The only three states in our survey with legislative term limits are Michigan, Colorado, and Maine. A term-limit law was passed in Washington as well, but it was struck down in early 1999.

49. For a discussion of the emergence of self-starters as candidates for congressional elections, see Thomas Kazee, ed., *Who Runs for Congress?* (Washington, D.C.:

CQ Press, 1994); and L. Sandy Maisel, Linda Fowler, Ruth Jones, and Walter Stone, "The Naming of Candidates: Recruitment or Emergence?" in *The Parties Respond*, ed. L. Sandy Maisel (Boulder, CO: Westview Press, 1990).

50. John Frendreis and Alan Gitelson, "Local Parties in the 1990s: Spokes in a Candidate-Centered Wheel," in *The State of the Parties*, 3rd ed., ed. John C. Green and Daniel M. Shea (Lanham Md.: Rowman & Littlefield Publishers, Inc.), 144.

51. Our survey included eleven different types of groups or individuals, including the broad category "Other."

3

THE AGENTS OF RECRUITMENT

In the summer of 1984, Ralph Wright, the Democratic minority leader of the Vermont House, decided that he should make a serious effort to increase the number of seats held by the house Democrats, who were outnumbered 85 to 65. The first step, he decided, was to recruit more and better Democratic candidates to run for the house. Wright and his assistant minority leader set off across the state, going from town to town in an effort to find persons who had some experience in public affairs and who might be persuaded to run. They learned that in districts that were overwhelmingly Republican recruiting was usually hopeless, and therefore pointless. In one such town, he says, "We spun our wheels in our effort to find a brave soul who would run on the Democratic ticket, but it was to no avail."[1] Wright learned the importance of studying past voting records in the district, which was not easy because at that time it was a struggle simply to access such records. Once Wright had located good candidates willing to run, he spent much of the fall giving them practical advice on how to run a campaign.[2]

This first recruiting effort was good enough to increase the number of Democratic seats to 72 out of 150. When the new legislature convened, Wright persuaded enough Republicans to support him in his race for speaker that he won by a 76 to 74 margin. Wright continued to go back on the road, in election after election, to recruit more good candidates. Each time, he said, "I begin recruiting for the next election from the day of my election as speaker." In the next three elections, 1986, 1988, and 1990, the Democrats came within one or two votes of a majority, and Wright continued to hold the speakership. In 1992 the Democrats won a solid majority in the house, and they continued to hold it through the 1990s.

Wright's story, in a very small state many years ago, is relevant today because it illustrates a number of aspects of the legislative recruitment process. His effort began at about the same time that many other leaders were beginning to systematically recruit candidates and raise money for them. Many state legislative leaders first did this in the mid-1980s. Wright, like many other leaders, took this initiative because the party balance in the house had in recent years grown close enough so that it was realistic to think a major effort could win a majority.

Wright learned, as others have, that to recruit candidates you have to develop good contacts at the local level, which usually requires personal visits from town to town. Wright did not have mathematical formulas or computer programs to calculate the party balance in each district; he had trouble enough getting his hands on district election data. But he quickly recognized, as others have, that it was important to target districts that might be winnable with the right candidate and enough effort. He recognized that there was simply no point in trying to find a candidate in really safe Republican districts where, even if a good candidate could be drafted, winning was virtually hopeless.

It is unusual for persons who have never given any thought to running for the legislature to be approached by party leaders. Most candidates first think of running on their own, perhaps when a vacancy occurs, and then are encouraged by a party or interest group leader to run. When recruiters come into a district, they begin asking questions about persons who have been active in politics, interest groups, or public affairs—some of whom may have held elected office or at least run for election. Mike Hubbard, profiled in this chapter (on pages 54–55), is a good example of a self-starter who later got party support. On the other hand, David Custer (profiled in Chapter 5), a relative newcomer to politics, was a reluctant candidate only after his wife decided her health was not good enough for her to run.

Ralph Wright, searching for candidates in districts where the party had never done any recruiting and where the Republicans at least gave the appearance of being in control, was looking for more than warm bodies. He wanted to find Democrats with some interest and experience in public affairs, whether or not they had ever thought of running for the legislature; and sometimes he could find them.

THE ROLE OF POLITICAL PARTIES AS RECRUITING AGENTS

Recruiting was traditionally the job of state and local party organizations, some of which were powerful enough to pick the candidates they wanted and make sure that those people got nominated. Candidates who had a strong record of service to the political party had the best chance of being supported by the party to run for public office. With the spread of the direct primary election to most states in the first half of the twentieth century, it became much more difficult for state and local parties to control the nomination. Their power began to decline, in part because patronage became a much weaker tool. Consequently, fewer parties were able to handpick the candidates to run for office.[3]

Despite these trends, recruitment should remain an important responsibility of political parties since their major function is to run candidates for public office and try to win elections. Obviously, political parties want to run candidates who have the best chance of being elected. The party may also prefer candidates who share its values and viewpoints, and who will be attractive to the individuals and interest groups that are predisposed to vote for that party.

There is an obvious linkage between the recruitment and nomination of candidates. If party leaders recruit the best candidate they can find, they want that candidate to get nominated. In fact, it may be difficult to persuade someone to run for office if the party can not help that person get nominated. The party can not guarantee nomination to its preferred candidate, but it may be able to provide tangible assistance to that candidate and perhaps discourage other candidates from running in the primary.

PARTY ORGANIZATIONS AND LEGISLATIVE CAMPAIGN COMMITTEES

Across the fifty states, there are three types of party organizations that are involved, to varying degrees, in recruiting candidates. At the state level, the state party organization or the senate and house legislative committees may play a role. In some states, both are involved in recruiting and work together; in other states, either the state organization or the legislative committees, but not both, recruit legislative candidates. Additionally some local parties are active in recruiting, sometimes working closely with the state party.

The state party organization has the general responsibility for recruiting and providing campaign support for its candidates in the state. It often runs, or at least organizes, programs that benefit all candidates, such as voter registration and get-out-the-vote programs. In some states, such as Arizona, Florida, Maine, and Tennessee, this is the organization that targets those legislative districts that are likely to be most competitive and tries to recruit good candidates for them. In other states, however, the state organization concentrates on more important races, for governor, other state offices, and U.S. senator and representative. It may not have enough time or resources to pay much attention to legislative races. Or the state party organization may provide particular services to support state legislative campaign committees that assume the primary responsibilities for recruiting and supporting legislative candidates— as in Indiana, Ohio, and Minnesota. If the party controls the governorship, the governor may decide how high a priority the state party organization should give to legislative races. The governor has a considerable interest in his party winning, or holding on to, a majority in the legislature.

A major innovation by state parties during the 1980s and 1990s was the development of legislative campaign committees, run by the party leaders. They have been active in recruiting legislative candidates and then providing financial support and other tangible campaign assistance to both incumbent

Candidate Profile

☑ **MIKE HUBBARD**, Republican candidate for Alabama House District 79, 1998

Mike Hubbard is a well-known local figure in the Auburn area. He is the President of Auburn Network, Inc., the company that owns the media rights for Auburn University football games and other sports. A graduate of the University of Georgia, he has a degree in broadcasting and considerable media savvy. He is thirty-six years old, energetic, successful, personable, and he was heavily recruited by the House GOP Caucus to run for this seat.

Although he has never run for elective state or local office before, Hubbard has always been interested in politics. In high school he was senior class president and he won the Georgia state title in the American Legion Oratorical Award. He has a cousin who served in the Georgia State Legislature. Hubbard produced radio spots for U.S. Congressman Bob Riley during the 1996 campaign. He also helped manage the Auburn University Athletic Department's Heisman Trophy campaign for Bo Jackson—which may be as close to a political campaign as anything in sports!

Hubbard and his wife, a professor at Auburn University, are strong Christians. "When I was deciding whether or not to run, I went back and forth for many months," Hubbard said. "Finally, my wife and I decided to prayerfully ask for guidance and also ask our family, pastor, and close friends to also pray for us to make the right decision. It was amazing how doors started to open for me at that point and I felt it was something I was being led to do."

His opponent, Jan Dempsey, had been elected mayor of the city of Auburn, Alabama for five terms. Having served in public office for eighteen years, she is one of the most successful female politicians in the state. Between them, Dempsey and Hubbard spent over $250,000 on this race.

The House Republican Caucus targeted this seat, which had been held for forty years by the same man, a Democrat. The district changed over time, and the GOP felt it was ripe for them. When the incumbent decided to retire, the Republican Caucus pushed Hubbard very hard to run. They invited him to Montgomery, the capital, to meet with Republican-oriented PACs. He also received advice and support from the state's GOP Congressional delegation. With a large campaign budget, Hubbard was able to do a series of direct mail campaigns and also had radio spots and some cable television ads.

The campaign was long and tough. Mike said he was "surprised by the games people play. People you think are your friends engage in whisper campaigns. It's tough. But my wife and I agreed when I decided to run that we weren't going to lose one friend over the campaign, because it's not worth it."

When asked if he would do it again, he laughed and said, "I don't know. It has been such an emotional roller coaster. The day my opponent got her forces out and covered the city with yard signs, I was so depressed. I thought, 'I'm going to get creamed.' But then the next day you bounce back and you feel you are going to win and you are on the top of the world."

Mike Hubbard won the election with 58 percent of the vote.

Hubbard with wife, Dr. Susan Hubbard, a professor at Auburn University in Nutrition and Food Science. The SGA recently recognized Dr. Hubbard as one of the outstanding faculty members on the Auburn campus.

MIKE HUBBARD IS THE
RIGHT CHOICE FOR
AUBURN STUDENTS
ON NOVEMBER 3RD

See Reverse Side For *10 Great Reasons* To Vote For Mike Hubbard As Your State Representative .

Mike
HUBBARD
STATE REPRESENTATIVE

The Mike Hubbard material is reprinted with the permission of Mike Hubbard.

and nonincumbent legislative candidates. In many states, the legislative campaign committees were developed to fill a vacuum left by the state party organization. The increasing costs of campaigns and the growing two-party competition in many legislative chambers also made these campaign committees more necessary. At first, priority was given to funding incumbent legislators, but soon the party leaders recognized the importance of recruiting and supporting nonincumbent candidates.[4]

There is evidence that at least three-fourths of the 196 legislative parties (excluding nonpartisan Nebraska) have active campaign committees; and in at least thirty-six states, three or usually all four of the legislative parties have such committees. Most of the legislatures that have few or no legislative campaign committees are in those southern states where the Republican party has been badly outnumbered by Democrats in the legislature until very recently.

The effort of legislative parties to recruit candidates, raise campaign finance funds, target districts, and allocate funds to candidates is largely carried out by the leaders of the legislative parties.[5] In addition to largely controlling the campaign finance committees, some legislative leaders operate their own political action committees (PACs), recruiting, raising funds, and allocating monies to candidates. This gives them somewhat greater flexibility in deciding how to allocate the funds. Although, strictly speaking, leadership PACs are not party organizations, in practice they are tools used by the leadership to recruit and support legislative candidates.

State party organizations, legislative campaign finance committees, and leadership PACs all raise a considerable proportion of their funds from interest group PACs. Because legislative leaders play a crucial role in deciding which bills will pass and which will be defeated, these leaders may be in a stronger position than state party organizations are to raise campaign funds from interest group PACs. However, if a party controls the governorship and the governor works closely with the state party organization, that body may be equally successful in attracting campaign funds from interest group PACs.

Occasionally there may be conflicts between the state party organizations and the legislative committees over how to allocate funds or which legislative candidate to support. The executive director of the House Democratic Campaign Committee in one state told us that there had been conflicts between the state and legislative Democratic organizations, but cooperation improved considerably when a former legislator who had headed the legislative campaign committee became chair of the state party. In some states, there is also occasional rivalry between a party's senate and house campaign committees because both are trying to recruit the same strong candidates or the senate committee is trying to recruit members of the house in a particular locality.

Some legislative campaign committees send field workers to help a newly recruited candidate run his or her campaign. Sometimes these advisors wind up irritating the candidate by the kind of advice offered or the style of the worker. One candidate in Washington state who was given a media adviser said, "They know how to run a campaign in King County but not necessarily in ... [my district]. They were too demanding and dogmatic about how to do it."

Local party organizations probably play a smaller role in recruiting and supporting legislative candidates than many of them used to.[6] There is a smaller proportion of well-organized, disciplined local party organizations than in the past. Moreover, since the 1960s when the courts began to require that legislative districts be based strictly on population, the boundaries of legislative districts are much less likely to coincide with the boundaries of counties and cities, making local parties less likely to feel responsible for supporting legislative candidates. Nevertheless, the state and legislative parties are dependent on local party leaders and elected officials for advice on finding potential candidates for the legislature. Some local parties still provide considerable funding to legislative candidates; and candidates generally draw most of their volunteer campaign workers from the pool of activists in the local party.

COMPETITION IN LEGISLATIVE DISTRICTS

From the political party's perspective, there are three kinds of legislative districts: those that the party usually wins, those where strong two-party competition is the norm, and those that the party seldom if ever wins. The party's recruiting job is different in the three districts.

In safe legislative districts, the party usually does not have to hunt for candidates. If the party's incumbent legislator is running again, there is seldom any opposition within the party; if there is, the party would normally support the incumbent. If the incumbent is not seeking reelection for that seat, there are likely to be several candidates running, because the seat appears to be a safe one. If this is the case, the party's job is to review the credentials of those who are running, determine who would make the best candidate, and if possible discourage other candidates. Even if the seat appears to be safe, the party does not want a weak candidate running who could lose if the other party puts up a particularly strong candidate. Moreover, the party does not want a candidate nominated who would be an embarrassment to the party even if he or she got elected.

In closely competitive districts, if the party does not have an incumbent running, there are likely to be several persons interested in running because there is a reasonable chance of winning. Because it is a close district, it is particularly important for the party to determine who would make the best candidate, to help that candidate get nominated, and if possible to prevent a divisive and expensive primary election.

In districts that have been controlled by the other party, often for many years, the job of recruiting is most difficult. Of course, it is hard to persuade someone to run for office when the chances of winning appear to be remote.

In such a district, there is unlikely to be a strong, active local party organization to help with recruiting. There are likely to be smaller numbers of persons in the party who have been active in politics or public affairs, and even fewer who have ever thought seriously of running for public office.

TARGETING DISTRICTS

It is obviously important for a political party to make judgments about the priorities for recruiting and supporting legislative candidates. The job of recruiting, if it is taken seriously, consumes lots of time and energy. Party leaders must often visit the district, talking to local leaders and then identifying and talking to prospective candidates. Moreover, as we have said, it is often necessary to provide a promising candidate with tangible campaign assistance in order to persuade him or her to run and to increase the chances of winning.

Party leaders agree that it is most important to recruit and support candidates in districts where neither victory nor defeat appears certain. This means working in competitive districts where the voters can be swayed by a particularly strong candidate. It also means working in districts that have been lost in the past but appear winnable if a good enough candidate can be found and supported.

For these reasons, political parties try to target districts as accurately as possible. Targeting may sound simple, but it is not. It is easy to look at the percentage by which the legislative seat was won by one party or the other in the last couple of elections, but these figures may be deceptive. The outcome of a legislative race, like any other election, depends in large part on two factors: what is sometimes called the "normal party vote," based on the party loyalties and turnout of voters in the district; and the strengths and weaknesses of the two candidates in the race.

As legislators in most states have grown more professional and experienced, and have developed greater political strength, many legislators have been able to win reelection rather comfortably in districts that are not traditionally safe for their party. The more strongly entrenched a legislator appears to be, the less likely it is that strong candidates will be willing to run against him or her in a general election, and this supports the myth that the incumbent is unbeatable.

A good example of a party taking seriously the job of targeting districts is the Republican party in Georgia.[7] They collect precinct-level data in the district on several other recent races, such as president, senator, governor, or other statewide office, and calculate an average party vote, so that they can compare this normal party vote with recent legislative elections. This helps the party determine what chances its candidate would have if the incumbent (of either party) were not running for reelection or if the incumbent of the other party were believed to be less popular because of his or her recent voting record or some other issue. If the results of a targeting vote analysis in a particular district are encouraging, party leaders can show these figures to a potential candidate and perhaps persuade him or her to run.

An essential step in making informed decisions about targeting districts is the collection and analysis of voting data on a variety of races in the district. Almost all party leaders pay careful attention to such information; but the data do not automatically determine the decision about recruiting and supporting a candidate in the district. Party leaders often emphasize that other factors are important, particularly the availability of a strong candidate, which sometimes is more important than voting data. An experienced legislative leader in Maryland says, "If I have the best candidate and he or she is willing to work hard, I think we will win." Leaders also need to pay attention to the strength or weakness of the other party's candidate in making a targeting decision. A California senate leader reports that in that state there are so many marginal districts (based on voting data) that other factors have to be taken into account in targeting. One such factor, of course, is the amount of money the party has to help fund candidates.

There are also various approaches to targeting strategy. The question is not which districts, but how many, should be targeted. For example, if there are one hundred members in the house, with fifty-five seats controlled by Democrats and forty-five by Republicans, and ten of the incumbents in each party are not seeking reelection, what might be the targeting strategies? The Republican targeting strategy will probably give high priority to recruiting good candidates for the ten seats where its incumbents are not running, because those seats are probably winnable but still vulnerable without an incumbent running. A second recruiting priority will probably be at least some of the ten Democratic seats with no incumbent running, since these are now open seats. For recruiting purposes, the Republican leaders might be able to rank, from highest to lowest priority, the sixty-five seats without a Republican incumbent running. But that does not answer the question of whether the party should concentrate on twenty, thirty, or forty districts, or try to recruit someone for all of these districts.

The closer the two-party balance, the greater likelihood that both parties will target a smaller proportion of seats, because partisan control of the chamber may depend largely on the outcome in a few districts. In the Washington state 1998 election, for example, the Democrats—needing only two more seats to take over the senate—targeted seven seats and won control of that chamber. They targeted ten seats in the house and won seven, gaining a tie in that chamber. Their victories came in some of the targeted seats plus a few others where they had not expected to win. In some states, a large proportion of seats appear very safe for one party, and therefore a smaller proportion of seats will be targeted by either party.

A party's targeting strategy may change from one election to the next, because of a change in leadership, because national trends shift in favor of a different party, or because of recent political history. A party that narrowly missed capturing some seats that appeared completely unwinnable and thus untargeted in one election may decide in the next election to expand the number of districts where it targets a seat and recruits aggressively.

Allocating financial resources among candidates is even more difficult. If the party has $300,000 available, does it spend all of it on the ten highest priority districts, or does it divide $200,000 among these ten and the remaining $100,000 among ten or fifteen districts with slightly lower priority? Setting recruiting priorities is less difficult than allocating resources, but there are costs involved in recruiting candidates because this process takes time and effort, and some of those recruited are going to insist that they need tangible support from the party if they are going to be candidates. Therefore party leaders have to make careful decisions about which districts and how many deserve a serious recruiting effort.

PARTY AID TO CANDIDATES

Parties often have to offer tangible aid to prospective candidates both to persuade them to run and to give them a realistic chance of winning. After the leaders have located a promising recruit, they strike a bargain with him. In the state of Washington, for example, the candidate is expected to make a firm commitment to devote a large amount of time to the campaign—often nearly full-time effort for four to six months—and to raise a large proportion of the funds needed for a viable campaign. In return, the party may contribute a substantial amount of funds and might provide a consultant to the candidate to help with the media and the mailings. The party also expects the candidate to provide frequent progress reports on money raised, doorbells rung, and so forth.

Mike Hubbard of Alabama, profiled on pages 54–55, provides a good example of how hard the party will work to encourage a strong candidate to run in a district it has targeted. The Republican party targeted an open seat long held by a Democrat in a district that was becoming more Republican. When they decided that Hubbard would make a strong candidate, the Republican legislative caucus pushed him very hard to run, introduced him to PACs that usually supported Republicans, and enlisted Republican legislators from his area to give him advice and support.

Adam Clemons is another example of an Alabama Republican who ran in a district where Democrats appeared to be losing their dominant position and who had considerable Republican assistance, though he eventually lost the district. Pat Owens, an Alabama Republican challenging an incumbent Democratic senator, is a long-time party worker recruited by the lieutenant governor, who promised him financial help from the party.

Another service the party can provide, closely linked to targeting, is helping the candidate find the best possible seat for which to run. This is particularly useful in a state like Washington, which has some multimember districts. A good example is Laura Ruderman, a Democratic legislative candidate in the state of Washington who originally planned to run for U.S. Congress. When another candidate filed for the congressional seat, the Democratic Party asked Ruderman to step aside and discussed possible legislative seats where she might run. When she expressed an interest in the 45th district, the party decided that this seat, which had been held by Republicans, might be winnable. She raised and spent $180,000—a huge amount for a first-time candidate, with about $40,000 coming from the party—and she won by 51 to 49 percent.

Parties usually provide significant help only when they decide that the seat is winnable, and therefore targeted, and they have a good candidate. Kathryn Haigh, a Democratic challenger in Washington, is a good example. She had elective experience as a school board member and was experienced in legislative politics. A number of party leaders urged her to run against the incumbent. The House Democratic Campaign Committee provided substantial funds, campaign help, and a consultant who helped her with mailings. She beat the incumbent by a 51 to 49 percent margin. Another Washington Democrat, who lost by a narrow margin to an incumbent, got lots of party help in a targeted race. This included cash, help in paying for mailings, a precinct analysis, a briefing book on the incumbent, polling in her district, and the help of a consultant.

Many candidates get very little help from the party because the party has not targeted the district. A Democratic candidate in Colorado was encouraged by the party to run against the incumbent, but received little tangible support because the party had not targeted the race. He understood the principle of targeting, but thought the party should "look to the future" and target more seats. Another Colorado Democrat got only very modest amounts of party money and assistance because the party was not targeting the race even though the candidate had run well once before against the incumbent and was now running in an open seat race.

In Alabama, a number of Democratic candidates said that they received little if any support from their party, not only because the party had failed to target their races but also because the state and local parties appeared too weak or disorganized to either recruit candidates or significantly assist them. One Democratic candidate for a senate seat reported that the local party committee not only made no effort to recruit a candidate for the seat but did not even call him back when he announced his candidacy. Another Alabama Democrat, an experienced local politician running for an open house seat, said that both the state and local Democratic parties were in disarray and provided very little help.

WHAT RECRUITERS LOOK FOR IN A CANDIDATE

When a state party leader tries to recruit a good candidate for a district, they have to rely heavily on people in the district, including the local party leaders and activists, local office holders, legislators in their party from nearby districts, and others who are active in a variety of organizations. They often visit the district in person. A legislative leader from Maine said, "I do an in-depth evaluation of the district, its voting patterns and its particular characteristics. I call a variety of individuals in the district and informally question people in the district to build a profile of a winner." A party leader in Kansas stated, "In order to identify potentially strong candidates in districts not already controlled by the party, we set up recruitment committees made up of local Democratic party activists, professional association members, and representatives of interest groups who know the area to recommend potential candidates."

Most party leaders want individuals who have a strong commitment to run and are willing to work hard in the campaign. As one leader put it, "Candidates must be willing to dedicate their time—and have the time—to do the job, both in the campaign and as a legislator."

One legislative campaign committee staff director describes how she recruits candidates:

> You start with folks who ran before and did a credible job, also with city council, county elected officials, local party activists, local labor union activists. You get outside the normal scene and search school boards and commissions, retired teachers, and firefighters. You are looking for people with good ties to the entire community, not just partisan ties. The potential candidate has to be someone the community likes and trusts, with the ability to network with others and especially to be willing to work hard in the campaign—fire in the belly.

Recruiters stress that a good candidate should have standing in the community; this means being well known, having a good reputation, and having a record of organizational leadership. A related, and very important point, is that a candidate should know the district well and share its views. A Michigan legislative leader describes how important it is to know the needs of the district in order to identify the best possible candidate:

> We would contact the party organizations in the district and have them help us with suggestions of individuals they think might be potential candidates. We also would visit with members of the community to get a feel for what they would like in a candidate and what issues are important to them and to the area. Then we would look for individuals in the district who might be able to address those issues and who might appeal to the voters and who would be able to muster the support of the local political leaders and organizations.

Experience in elective office is considered to be an asset, but in reality many persons who run for the legislature have not held any other elective office. Personal qualities are also important: good judgment, intelligence, competence, integrity, and specifically, a record free of scandals.

Recruiters often mention how important it is that a candidate be willing and able to raise campaign money. This is one of the best indicators of whether the candidate has a realistic chance of winning. Even though party leaders can help a candidate raise money, and sometimes provide funding or campaign assistance, they can not do everything.

A number of party leaders have emphasized that, when it comes to issues and ideology, the priority is to find a candidate who is typical of the district. A Democratic legislator in Maine said, "Instead of looking for someone whose views are typical of the state party, but who may be too liberal or too conservative for the district, it is important to find someone who can win in the district." In similar fashion, the former Democratic speaker of the Wisconsin House told us, "We do not have a litmus test on issues or ideology for recruiting. We never try to pick someone who is more liberal or more conservative. Any Democrat will vote to organize with the Democrats on the first day of the session; that is the important thing." A Democratic leader in Republican Utah had a similar comment: "A person with moderate stands on issues is helpful because in a very conservative Republican state a very liberal Democrat would be a sacrificial lamb."

Kathryn Haigh is a good example of a strong candidate. She had lengthy experience in community affairs, including serving several terms on a school board; she had represented an interest group in the legislature; and she was energetic and articulate. Not surprisingly, Democratic leaders eagerly recruited her.

Adam Clemons, an Alabama Republican, is a good example of a candidate with political experience. He was only twenty-one when he ran for an open house seat in 1998. But at age seventeen he had worked actively for the legislator against whom he was now running, and therefore he knew the district well. He had established many contacts with Republican leaders, planned his campaign strategy carefully, and knew how to run a professional campaign.

THE LINK BETWEEN RECRUITING AND NOMINATING

If the party recruits the best available candidate for the legislature, it wants him or her to get nominated, and the candidate may insist on party help prior to the nomination. The problem, of course, is that the party can not directly control nominations.

In a district that is usually controlled by a particular party, there is more likely to be strong competition in that party's primary because the chance of winning the general election is greater. In a district that is not dominated by either party, it is more important for the party to run the strongest candidate, the one most likely to be elected. These are the districts most likely to be targeted, and these are the ones where the party will probably make the greatest effort to prevent a contested primary or to influence the outcome if there is a contest.

It is especially important for a party to influence open primaries, to prevent independents or members of the other party (who can vote in either party's open primary) from determining who will be nominated. It is even more important for the party to try to influence nominations in states like Washington, Minnesota, or New York, where there is only a short time between the primary and general elections and therefore a short time to heal differences if the primary is bitterly contested.

Some political parties make a direct effort to influence the choice of a nominee by making a formal endorsement of a candidate; in the case of legislative candidates, these would be made by district caucuses—though these decisions might be ratified by a state convention. Such endorsements occur in one or both parties in about a dozen states, and leadership endorsements are frequent in several others.

Incumbent legislators are almost always endorsed and almost always win renomination. But nonincumbent legislative candidates who win endorsement are often opposed, and endorsement does not guarantee victory. Jim Finley, of Colorado, is an example of a candidate who successfully challenged the endorsee (see profile on pages 66–67). He had the support of a gun-owner's interest group. But his ties to the party were so weak that, in the party's district caucus, he not only failed to win the largest vote, he was unable to win the minimum 30 percent of the vote needed to automatically qualify for the primary ballot. But he got on the ballot by petition, campaigned intensively, and beat two other candidates to win the nomination. Interestingly, he received financial and other assistance from the state and local party in the general election and narrowly won.

Interest groups that are supporting a candidate different from the one supported by party leaders may concentrate their efforts in the primary election; but, in a state like Colorado that holds endorsing caucuses for legislative candidates, these groups may try to win control of the caucus. In Colorado, where the caucuses are important, religious right groups have tried to "stack" the Republican caucuses with their members, and have also organized training sessions to teach their members about techniques that may help them to win control of the caucus.

Challengers to the candidate recruited by party leaders may be supported by a particular interest group, as was Jim Finley, and/or by another wing of the party, such as someone promoted by a labor union in the Democratic party or by the religious right in the Republican party. The more deeply divided the party, the more difficulty a party-recruited candidate may face in winning nomination. Sue Singer, a Washington businesswoman who had been twice elected to city council, illustrates the perils a recruit faces in a deeply divided party (see profile on pages 68–69). Singer appeared to have all the qualifications a party would want, and in fact both parties tried to recruit her. She turned down the Democrats, met with high-ranking Republican leaders, and agreed to be a Republican candidate for the Washington House. But there were deep divisions between the state-level Republican leaders and local precinct leaders who were supporting a more conservative candidate. Singer lost to that candidate in the Washington blanket primary, but then the conservative candidate lost in the general election.

There are several conditions under which the candidates whom a party has encouraged to run have a good chance of being nominated. The party may provide enough tangible assistance to its candidates early in the race that other candidates are discouraged from running. In a district that is not relatively safe for one party, outside candidates may be less likely to challenge the inside candidate in a primary.

Candidates supported by the party may have the best chance of winning nomination if they have been active in the party and worked for its candidates, thereby acquiring not only experience but also a number of contacts among party activists. One example is a Colorado Republican who is pro-choice and had an opponent supported by the Christian Coalition. She had experience managing campaigns and winning school board elections, and she had a long record of party activity, factors that helped her win about a 60 percent majority in both the endorsing caucus and the primary. Another Colorado Republican has been active in the state party organization and in running training programs for party activists. As an insider, he was able to win a three-way primary. A Washington Republican who was party chair of the district actively sought to recruit candidates, but agreed to run herself when it became clear she was the strongest candidate. Because she was well known to activists and had worked to mend fences in the party, she was able to avoid primary opposition entirely.

A SOUTHERN PERSPECTIVE ON RECRUITING AND TARGETING

Republicans in the South have demonstrated how targeting and recruitment can transform a state legislature's politics. The Democratic party held large and overwhelming majorities in most southern legislatures for most of the twentieth century. To overcome this, the Republican party in the 1980s and 1990s began to vigorously recruit more and better candidates, and it targeted districts where its efforts would be most productive.

Table 3.1 (on page 67) shows the effect of the Republican strategy in ten southern states. During the 1970s, the Republicans contested only about 45 percent of all state legislative seats in the South. In the 1980s, they contested a slightly higher percentage of seats, and by the 1990s they were contesting over 60 percent of the seats. Moreover, the Republicans were increasingly astute in their targeting of specific seats; while they won only about 18 percent of the seats in the 1970s, they were winning over 30 percent of the seats by the end of the next decade. And in the 1990s, they won an average of about 40 percent of the seats. In other words, Republicans were not only recruiting more southern legislative candidates, but also recruiting better candidates and focusing on districts where they had the potential for winning.

☑ JIM FINLEY,* candidate for the Colorado House, 1998

Jim Finley is an unlikely candidate who took an unlikely path to the general election candidacy. A native of a midwestern state, he moved to Colorado about a decade ago. He is a line supervisor in a factory, and attended school at night to earn a college degree. Jim's political activism was fueled by a specific issue: gun owner's rights. He is a member of the Centennial Gun and Rifle Organization. He has "been involved in firearms issues, and lobbied as a citizen lobbyist on a few bills." He may be the closest thing we have to someone who was primarily recruited (or at least supported) by an interest group.

Finley's route to candidacy was unique. Colorado has an unusual primary system. Candidates must receive at least 30 percent of the votes in district caucus meetings (called district assemblies) in order to have their name placed on the primary ballot. Clearly not part of the mainstream network of the political party (what Jim called "the same old machine"), he failed to get the requisite 30 percent of the assembly delegate votes. There is, however, a rarely-used mechanism whereby anyone who did not reach the necessary assembly vote threshold can still get on the ballot via petition. In order to qualify by this route, the petition must be signed by several hundred individuals. With support from the Centennial Gun and Rifle Organization members, Jim Finley managed to get the necessary signatures and successfully petition onto the primary ballot.

Once on the ballot, Finley worked diligently to get the nomination. Claiming that the assembly experience was a "wake-up call," he worked the district assiduously before the primary. He spent over $6,000 and pounded the pavement. He was the only primary candidate in his race to do a literature drop. To the surprise of many, he won the primary over several other candidates.

Building on the name-recognition and momentum he developed during the primary, Jim continued to campaign door-to-door. He walked the district from 5:00 to 8:00 P.M. every day after work, and from noon to 7:00 P.M. on weekends. He says, "It takes a total commitment in terms of getting out there, willing to learn about all the issues. It takes a lot of your time—it's ruining my hunting season!"

*Note: Because of the sensitive nature of the firearms issue in Colorado, we have changed the candidate's name and some of the particulars of the race.

In addition to walking the district, Finley used direct mail. His campaign manager (also a member of the Centennial Gun and Rifle Organization) happens to be a computer programmer and fashioned an effective direct mail system. Although Jim was clearly a party-outsider in the primary, once he won the primary election, the party supported him. He received several thousand dollars from the party's legislative caucus, and he had some local party help with his literature drops. He spent less than $20,000 in the campaign; his opponent spent about the same amount.

Overall, Jim thinks the campaign experience has been mixed. He is bothered by the fact that "people aren't very interested in the system. It is very frustrating." On the other hand, he has discovered "there are a lot of good people, too." When asked if he would do it again, he said, "I'm not sure."

Jim Finley narrowly won the general election, receiving slightly over 50 percent of the total vote.

TABLE 3.1 PROPORTION OF SEATS IN THE STATE HOUSES THAT WERE CONTESTED AND WON BY REPUBLICAN CANDIDATES IN TEN SOUTHERN AND BORDER STATES

ELECTION PERIOD	PERCENT OF SEATS CONTESTED	PERCENT OF SEATS WON	PERCENT OF CANDIDATES WHO WON
1968–1971	45%	18%	40%
1972–1975	50	19	37
1976–1979	43	17	38
1980–1983	48	22	45
1984–1987	47	27	57
1988–1991	55	33	60
1992–1993	60	35	58
1994	62	42	68
1995–1996	73	44	60

Note: The ten states are Alabama, Florida, Georgia, Kentucky, Mississippi, North Carolina, South Carolina, Tennessee, Texas, and Virginia.
Source: computed by the authors.

Candidate Profile

☑ SUE SINGER, Republican candidate for the Washington House District 31, seat 1, 1998

At the beginning of 1998, Sue Singer liked her chances. She was well connected in her community, a moderate, and a lifelong resident of the area. She owned a small sign business, was involved in the local chamber of commerce, and was active in local service organizations. She had been elected to the city council in Auburn (Washington, not Alabama), a suburb southeast of Seattle. (City council elections in Washington are nonpartisan.) Her husband had served on the local school board for twelve years.

When the 1998 election season began, Sue Singer was recruited by *both* major political parties. The Democrats came calling first, but she declined because, as a local businesswoman, "I felt my philosophy was more in tune with the Republican party than the Democrats."

When the incumbent in the house seat decided not to seek reelection, his former campaign manager called Sue and urged her to run. She met with the House GOP Legislative Caucus committee chair and three GOP state representatives. On April 28 she announced her candidacy. On the same day, another GOP candidate announced. Although she faced several opponents in the primary, Sue was confident of her chances. What she had not reckoned on was the bitter ideological factionalism characteristic of the Republican party in some local areas in Washington. What she learned was that "the House Republican Organizing Committee (the LCC) is totally out of touch with some of the local PCOs (Precinct Committee Organizations)."

In early summer a new candidate—one supported by the religious right—emerged. He also happened to be the son of a state senator, a conservative Republican woman with great influence with some of the local precinct committee officers. Later, a fourth GOP candidate joined the race. The primary battle was heated and very bitter. Singer described the district caucus meetings, where the various candidates in the primary would appear before the local party faithful, as "confrontational" and often full of "personal attacks from the precinct committee officers."

The primary in Washington is a "blanket primary"—all the candidates (regardless of party affiliation) appear on the same ballot. Voters can vote for any one candidate. The candidates with the most votes from each party then face each other in the general election. In the House District 31 (seat 1) primary, the senator's son got the Republican plurality of votes, with 30.3 percent. Singer polled the second-largest percentage at 22.6 percent. The leading Democrat got 20 percent of the primary vote. The primary was so divisive that none of the losing Republican candidates would endorse the GOP primary winner. The divisiveness of the Republicans helped the

Democrats. In the general election, the Democratic candidate—who only received one-fifth of the primary votes—beat the senator's son.

Sue Singer is a woman who was emotionally battered by this experience. She spent $58,000 in the primary campaign, and would undoubtedly have won the general election. But she was caught in the internecine war of the local factional politics of her party. In reflecting back on the campaign, she says, "The bottom line is that I failed to get the moderates out to vote and the ... [the opposition] succeeded in rallying the far right elements of the party."

She is completely turned off by party politics. She intends to run for reelection to her (nonpartisan) city council seat and to stay active in the community, but claims "I will never run for the state legislature again."

Sue Singer lost the primary election by 8 percentage points. In 1999 she was reelected (unopposed) to the Auburn city council.

SUE SINGER

For State House • GOP • 31st District

THOUGHTFUL, DEDICATED, AND CARING LEADERSHIP WE CAN COUNT ON!

"Over 20 years, I've met a lot of neighbors, made a lot of friends and had the pleasure of helping a lot of people. That's the part I love most about being involved in our community – the people. As your state representative, listening to your thoughts, ideas and concerns will always be my top priority. I would appreciate your vote on September 15."

Sue

There are some variations among southern state Republican parties on the number of legislative candidates running and the number getting elected that suggest some differences in recruiting and targeting strategy. Some parties have continued to increase the number of candidates that they run, while others appear to have become more selective about the districts they target, winning an increasing number of seats without large increases in the number of candidates running.

Texas is the best example of a state where the Republicans have increased their victories more than they have increased candidates. Between 1968–1970 and 1994–1997, the proportion of seats Republicans contested rose from 43 to 66 percent; the number won rose from 6 to 43 percent; and the percentage of candidates winning rose from 14 to 66 percent. Beginning in the early 1980s, the Republicans obviously became more selective about where they ran candidates, and must have put more resources into those races. The political coordinator of the Texas Republican party attributed this success to their targeting and recruitment strategy.[8]

Alabama is a southern state that lagged behind most others in recruiting candidates and winning legislative elections. From 1960 through 1967, there was only one Republican in the Alabama legislature. But eventually the Republican party learned how to target and recruit; from the 1986 elections to 1994, the number of Republicans elected to the house doubled, with only a modest increase in the contested races. In the 1994 through 1998 elections, the proportion of Republicans elected to the house averaged about one-third.

RECRUITING BY INTEREST GROUPS

Recruitment is not one of the major functions of interest groups, in contrast to parties, but some candidates mentioned linkages to groups that played a role in their decision to run for office.

Some interest groups are closely linked to political parties. Republican leaders often work closely, at both the state and national level, with such groups as the Christian Coalition, right-to-life groups, anti-tax organizations, the National Rifle Association and its state counterparts, and a variety of business groups. The Democratic party is linked to labor unions, teachers' organizations, women's groups and pro-choice organizations, some environmental groups, and various ethnic and racial groups. The staff director of the House Democratic Campaign Committee in one state identified a number of interest group PACs that are "funding partners" of the Democratic party. They make substantial contributions to the party and work with it in recruiting candidates and deciding which potential candidates should be encouraged to run in targeted races.

When party leaders are looking for potential candidates in a particular city or county, it is natural for them to consider persons who have been active in the groups that are close to the party. Republican recruiters consider persons who have held office in business organizations like the Chamber of Commerce or persons who have campaigned for a referendum to cut spending or taxes at the local level. Democratic recruiters sometimes turn to those who are actively involved in a local labor union or women who have been active in pro-choice groups. This is natural because a number of party leaders and activists have been very involved in interest groups and became active in parties and election campaigns in order to work for the policy goals promoted by those groups. The Alabama Education Association, for example, is active in recruiting candidates to run in that state.[9] When political parties are divided over ideology and issues, it is often because many of their active members have links to interest groups. Some groups encourage their active members to run for office and, sometimes, contested primaries are really battles between candidates belonging to different and conflicting interest groups.

Rich Hildreth, a Democrat who ran for the Washington House, was a very active member of a labor union and a party activist (see profile on pages 72–73). He served as party chair of his legislative district and decided to become a candidate. During the campaign, union members formed the core of his campaign organization. On the Republican side, Mike Hubbard, profiled earlier in this chapter, had very strong support from the leaders of the House Republican Campaign Committee, and also had support from the religious right.

On the other hand, Jim Finley, also profiled earlier, had his base of support in a gun owner's group in Colorado. He was an active member and he was able to enlist other members to work in his campaign. He had not been active in his party, finished third in the party's caucus vote, and had to get petitions signed to get on the primary ballot.

Lynda Straub, an Alabama Democrat, is another example of a candidate recruited by members of an interest group. As a businesswoman, she was very active in the local Chamber of Commerce, and was persuaded by associates in the Chamber to run for the state legislature. Billy John White had long been active in Democratic politics and had served in elective office in a small Alabama town. But the local party provided him with little support when he ran for an open house seat in 1998, and much of his support in a losing effort came from the Alabama Education Association. Other Alabama Democrats with little party support turned to labor groups like the State Employees Association and the AFL-CIO.

A number of Alabama Republican candidates received support from (and perhaps were recruited by) the Christian Coalition. One such candidate won a seat in a Birmingham suburb by defeating the Republican incumbent in the primary. He credited members of his church with playing a major role in his campaign. Another Alabama Republican with ties to the religious right reports that he first gave serious thought to running for the legislature at a

Candidate Profile

☑ RICHARD HILDRETH, Democratic candidate for the Washington House District 25, seat 1, 1998

Rich Hildreth is an electrician, a strong union man in a state, Washington, in which organized labor has long played an important political role. Several members of the Washington state legislature are union members. Like most union activists, Hildreth is a Democrat. His father was also actively involved in the labor union movement. Rich is in his mid-thirties. He and his wife have two young daughters. He teaches a class for the International Brotherhood of Electrical Workers (IBEW) on political involvement—a course designed to motivate union members to become more politically active. He serves on the Parks and Recreation Board in his hometown of Pacific. He is also on the King County Labor Council Board.

In 1998, Rich Hildreth beat another Democrat in the primary for the right to face a popular Republican incumbent, Joyce MacDonald, in the general election. In December of 1996, Hildreth was elected the Democratic Party Chair for House District 25. As Legislative District Chair, one of his tasks was to recruit candidates to run in the district, and, by the spring of 1998, he had decided he himself would run. He announced on April 3 and soon thereafter met with the staff director for the Democratic House Campaign Committee. One of his first acts was to seek the endorsement of the various union groups and PACs.

Hildreth characterized his core campaign group as "labor people." He received over half his contributions from labor PACs and the Democratic party. As a "working stiff," he found it difficult to juggle the campaign and his job. He worked full time on his regular job until Labor Day, then took a leave of absence to work on the campaign. Because of the peculiarities of Washington electoral politics, a campaign that does not hit its stride until Labor Day is at a tremendous disadvantage. There are two reasons for this. First, Washington has one of the latest primaries in the nation; in 1998 the primary election was held on September 15. Second, Washington is one of a handful of states making a concerted effort to permit its citizens easy access to voting by mail (traditionally known as absentee balloting). Mail ballots are usually sent out in mid-October, about three weeks prior to the general election. In some Washington state legislative districts, as many as 40 or 50 percent of all ballots in 1998 were cast by mail. The upshot is that a great deal of the campaigning must be done prior to the delivery of mail ballots.

Nonetheless, even with the late start to his campaign, Hildreth managed to ring over 15,000 doorbells. He had planned to send out four mailings to voters in the district, but he only had enough money for two mailings. Money was a scarce resource in his campaign, and Rich's wife served as his campaign treasurer. Hildreth spent about $28,000, only about half what his opponent was able to raise and spend. He was not able to hire a campaign manager.

When asked what he learned from this experience, Hildreth said, "I learned to be flexible, I learned to listen to people. I feel I grew a lot as a person." Although he was defeated, Rich plans to run again.

Rich Hildreth lost his election, 43 to 57 percent.

ELECT
RICHARD   *Working for Working Families*

HILDRETH

State Representative ••• 25th District ••• Position 1 ••• Democrat

QUALITY SCHOOLS:

I will work with parents, educators and community leaders to ensure our children have strong, safe and effective schools.

I will work with state officials, and business and labor leaders to find creative ways to restore funding to our schools without adding to our property taxes.

QUALITY COMMUNITIES:

I will work with citizens, property owners and business and development groups to develop a proactive plan for improving our infrastructure.

I will work with local prosecutors and police departments to develop criminal justice programs, including juvenile justice and community outreach, i.e. "Safe Streets".

QUALITY GOVERNMENT:

I will personally hold myself and my office accountable to be responsive to constituent's needs and concerns.

I will push for using common sense in forecasting and developing our state's budget. If our families must live within their means, so must our government.

Paid for by Committee to Elect Richard Hildreth, D
PO Box 251, Pacific, WA 98047-0251 (253) 274-1870

The Richard Hildreth material is reprinted with the permission of Richard Hildreth.

Promise-Keepers meeting. He also had a base of support among home-builders and realtors, and received help from their PACs, as well as some party funding.

In Alabama several predominantly black groups recruit and support African-American candidates for legislative as well as local office. By distributing sample ballots with their endorsed candidates highlighted, they also provide support in the African-American community for white candidates whom they believe will support the interests of African-Americans. They make endorsements in both primaries and general elections, and such endorsements can be crucial. In some areas of Alabama, African-American voters are likely to constitute a majority of votes in Democratic primaries because so many white Democrats have defected to the Republican party.

To summarize, political parties in recent years have become increasingly active in recruiting candidates for state legislatures. Their major purpose is to find the strongest available candidate in districts where the race is likely to be close. This includes districts with an open seat as well as those where the incumbent—either theirs or the other party's—is considered vulnerable. The parties look for candidates who have some experience in politics or public affairs, even if they have not actually held public office. They are particularly interested in candidates who can raise money. The parties make their recruiting decisions carefully because candidates in close races need tangible help from the party, and the party's resources are limited. The pragmatic strategy is to target only certain seats, and this means that parties leave some districts either uncontested or with only a weak candidate who gets little or no support from the party organization.

NOTES

1. Ralph Wright, *All Politics is Personal* (Manchester Center, Vt.: Marshall Jones Co., 1996), 62.
2. Wright, *All Politics is Personal.*
3. Malcolm E. Jewell and Sarah M. Morehouse, *Political Parties and Elections in American States*, 4th ed. (Washington, D.C.: CQ Press, 2000), Chap. 4.
4. Anthony Gierzynski, *Legislative Party Campaign Committees in the American States* (Lexington: University Press of Kentucky, 1992).
5. Gierzynski, *Legislative Party Campaign Committees in the American States.*
6. John Frendreis, Alan R. Gitelson, Shannon Jenkins, and Douglas D. Roscoe, "Candidate Emergence in State Politics" (Paper presented at the Annual Meeting of the Western Political Science Association, Seattle, Wash., March, 1999).
7. Charles Bullock III and David Shafer, "Party Targeting and Electoral Success," *Legislative Studies Quarterly* 22 (1997): 573–584.
8. William Cassie, "More May Not Always Be Better: Republican Recruiting Strategies in Southern Legislative Elections," *American Review of Politics* 15 (1994): 141–155.
9. Alan Ehrenhalt, *The United States of Ambition* (New York: Random House, 1992).

THE CANDIDATE AND THE CAMPAIGN

Campaigns in the United States today are characterized as "candidate-centered," meaning that each candidate must assemble his or her own campaign and fundraising team. The rise in candidate-centered campaigns and elections corresponds to the decline of political parties as the controlling forces in American politics.[1] The description of campaigns and elections as "candidate-centered" is especially apt for national elections; it has a more limited application to state legislative races.[2] For one thing, state legislative incumbents do not enjoy the extensive perquisites of office available to the average member of Congress. In some states, for example, legislators do not have personal staff. More important, state legislative districts are almost everywhere much smaller than congressional districts. While the average congressional district contains close to 600,000 people, in only a few states do legislative districts for the lower chamber contain even as many as 100,000 people.[3] There are over 7,400 state legislators in the United States, and approximately 1,800 (about 24 percent) of them represent districts with populations of 100,000 or more.[4] In thirty-one states, district size for the lower chamber is less than 45,000. In a few states, such as Maine, Montana, and Wyoming, there are fewer than 9,000 people per house district. There are fewer than 4,000 people in the Vermont and New Hampshire house districts.

Not only are there huge variations from state to state in the size of the districts, but there also are substantial differences even within a state in the character of the districts (metropolitan, suburban, rural, or a mix of types). In Minnesota, for example, the smallest state legislative district in geographic size is 6 square miles while the largest district is 4,760 square miles.[5] The former is a densely populated urban district in the Minneapolis area; the latter is in an extremely rural and sparsely-populated area in the northern region of the state. Clearly, the nature of campaigning—of reaching potential voters— is very different in these two cases.

What are the implications of the smaller district size for state legislative campaigns? Perhaps the most important consequence is that the ability to use extensive advertising through the electronic media is limited in most state legislative races. About 90 percent of U.S. Senate candidates and about 70 percent of U.S. House campaigns use television.[6] But television campaigns are not part of most state legislative races. Candidates for the Texas House of Representatives spent less than 9 percent of their voter contact budget on television, and about 9 percent on radio. In Kansas, only about 6 percent of the campaign expenditures went to radio ads, and less than 2 percent to television.[7] Most state legislative candidates do not make heavy use of the electronic media, particularly television, because state legislative districts do not generally correspond to media markets.[8] Consider, for example, the situation of a candidate running for the Missouri House of Representatives from a district in the Kansas City area. The Kansas City television market covers over two million people. Because the market has the potential to reach so many viewers, the cost of advertising time is relatively high. Each state legislative house district in Missouri contains fewer than fifty thousand people. To buy time on a Kansas City television station means that an extraordinary majority of the viewers (over 95 percent) are not in the candidate's legislative district. In fact, over 25 percent of the television audience doesn't even live in the same state, since about five hundred thousand people in the Kansas City media market actually live across the river in the state of Kansas! For the candidate, spending money on television advertising would be extraordinarily inefficient.

State legislative candidates in large metropolitan areas rarely find television a cost-effective way to reach potential voters. On the other hand, candidates running in more rural districts where the population is more dispersed may find that they would have to advertise on television stations in several different markets in order to reach the voters in their district. For perhaps 70 percent of the state legislative candidates, such an overlap is not very good and, consequently, advertising on commercial television is not a reasonable option.

This applies especially to regular broadcast television. In some instances, cable television is a viable option for candidates because the advertising costs are generally less, depending on the program on which the candidate's ad appears. Yet the audience market share is significantly less for almost all cable television programming, so one is still confronted with the cost-effectiveness issue. Nonetheless, cable television now appears to be a more prevalent medium for state legislative campaign ads than regular broadcast television. In Florida, for example, state legislative candidates regularly buy at least some advertising time on cable television.

Generally, the cost-benefit equation works out better for state senate candidates than for house candidates because the districts are usually larger. One California senator from San Diego, where the media market and the senate district are somewhat congruent, spent between $125,000 and $150,000 on a television blitz during the last week of the campaign. But for many state senate candidates, the costs of television advertising are simply too high for the anticipated return in terms of the target audience reached.

The other major constraint on the use of television is, of course, money. Candidates with larger budgets are more likely to be able to afford to use the airways, even if part of the advertising is "wasted" on those outside the district. Candidates with less than $50,000 in their campaign fund rarely use television; candidates with more money are more likely to purchase television time for campaign ads.[9] Of course, most state legislative candidates—and especially most nonincumbent legislative candidates—are not able to raise $50,000, and therefore are not likely to run television ads.[10]

Because most state legislative campaigns do not use television or even radio advertisements to the extent found in congressional or statewide races, and because the number of voters one needs to reach is usually much smaller, state legislative campaigns are different than those found in the more visible races. State legislative races tend to be fought doorstep-to-doorstep and mailbox-by-mailbox. And for many of these candidates, like Dave Custer of Colorado (see Candidate Profile on pages 78–79), this is their first experience in organizing a campaign.

GETTING PREPARED

Inexperienced candidates tend to underestimate the work involved in running a campaign. Often the novice thinks all he has to do is announce his candidacy, make up a few yard signs, and wait for the campaign contributions and volunteer supporters to come flowing in. Such a candidate is in for a shock. Conducting a good political campaign involves managing a complex set of tasks and it means a lot of hard work. Many of the candidates we interviewed made statements like, "I had no idea what I was getting into" or "I wish I knew earlier what I know now." Most campaigns proceed through three basic phases: the organizing phase, the fundraising and endorsement phase, and the voter contact phase.

THE ORGANIZING PHASE

Campaigns do not run themselves. Once the candidates decide they want to run, they must begin to put together a campaign plan and organization. Inexperienced candidates often underestimate the importance of these early steps.

☑ **DAVE CUSTER**, Republican candidate for the Colorado Senate District 24, 1998

Dave Custer is a shy, quiet man, who does not seem comfortable as a public figure, and was a rather reluctant candidate. He ran as the GOP candidate for the open senate seat in a district that leans toward the Democratic party. A former high school mathematics teacher, he is in his early sixties and has been looking forward to retiring soon from his job as an engineer for Bell Laboratories.

"About seven or eight years ago, I realized that complaining about politicians wasn't getting anything done. My wife and I decided to get involved; we went to a local Republican caucus meeting. There was hardly anybody there, and we wound up as delegates to the County Republican Assembly and my wife wound up as a delegate to the state convention."

After that, the Custers worked as volunteers for a congressional candidate. Custer's wife was especially active politically and, in fact, it was she who was originally the candidate in this race. She attended an invitation-only, GOP-sponsored candidate management school—150 hours of training sessions—for prospective candidates and campaign managers. After attending these sessions, she realized that her poor health would prevent her from being a candidate. She and the GOP county chair talked Dave into running.

Although the local party encouraged him to run, and even though Custer told them he "wasn't going to be a sacrificial lamb," it is clear that he did not get much assistance from the party. Neither the state nor local party provided him with much financial help. He raised only a few thousand dollars and could not afford any mailings.

The county party provided him with a voter identification list, and precinct captains helped put up some of his yard signs. But his was basically a solitary campaign. He took the entire month of October off from work to campaign, and walked the district, ringing doorbells. He concentrated on the newer housing developments in the area, hoping to register new voters in the area as he talked with them. He found the campaigning interesting but hard: "I used to take the politicians' statements about how hard they worked with great skepticism, but I've never worked harder in my life than in this campaign."

His greatest disappointment was the reaction of his co-workers when he announced he was going to run: "I've worked with some of these people for seventeen years. The day I told them I was going to run, some of them starting treating me different—distancing themselves from me, making jokes about 'Dave's a politician now.' That really hurt."

When asked if he would make the same decision to run, if he had it to do over again, he said, "Ask me in November, I hate to lose."

Dave Custer lost the election, 44 to 56 percent.

☑ Vote for

Dave

Custer

Citizen Candidate for State Senate
Not a Professional Politician

Dave will work for:
☺ Better Schools
☺ Better Roads
☺ Lower Taxes
☺ Smaller Less Intrusive Government

Paid for by The Committee To Elect Dave Custer, Karen Allen, Treasurer

The Dave Custer material is reprinted with the permission of Dave Custer.

CANDIDATE TRAINING SCHOOLS

Where does one go to find out how to run a campaign? There are, in fact, several universities that now offer graduate degrees in campaign management, but these programs are usually too long (a year or two) and expensive for most potential state legislative candidates. But political party organizations in some states are now conducting "campaign schools" or "training institutes" for potential candidates. Usually, these campaign management schools are sponsored by the state party organization, but in some places the county party may even conduct such workshops. These training sessions range from brief, one-day sessions covering the bare essentials to the more extensive and sophisticated workshops that may be held a few days each month, extending over several months. Often, the potential candidates must pay a fee of several hundred dollars to attend these longer sessions, but they usually find them worthwhile.

The political parties are not the only groups that conduct such training, however. Organizations such as *Campaigns & Elections Magazine*, the National Women's Political Caucus and the Southwest Voter Registration Project (a group devoted to increasing the political involvement of Hispanics) also offer campaign management workshops, but they are often held out of a candidate's state and are more expensive to attend.

Scaring off Potential Opponents

It is well known that congressional incumbents often build up large campaign war chests in order to discourage potential challengers. If the incumbent has hundreds of thousands of dollars already on hand, strategic politicians are less likely to enter the race. State legislative incumbents may engage in this "pre-emptive fundraising" strategy as well.

Our focus, however, is *nonincumbent* candidates. By definition, such candidates are either challenging an incumbent or running for an open seat. In open-seat races, it is unlikely that a candidate can scare off general election competition. But they may be able to dissuade primary election competition and thus be able to conserve precious resources for the general election campaign. The most effective way to do this is to announce your candidacy early, and then aggressively seek to establish a strong campaign organization. For example, one Colorado candidate said that as soon as she decided to run, she began telephoning people active in her local party as well as influential people in the community. The idea was to "get the word out" that she was organized early and would be a formidable opponent to anyone else considering running in the primary. At the same time, astute candidates will get their campaign organizations lined up. This means finding a campaign manager and treasurer. Ideally, it also means building a base of volunteer workers. In most state legislative districts, there is a limited supply of people who are willing to devote their time and energy to campaign work. By "capturing the volunteer market," the candidate can further discourage primary opposition. One Republican candidate in Washington, where the primary election is not until September, said, "I got in the race early. The primary is really decided in January or February if you are a good candidate and well organized."

Of course, if the candidate can generate a lot of money early, or is wealthy enough to be able to bankroll the campaign on her own, she may deter other potential candidates. Most potential donors, however, are hesitant to contribute money in a primary race.

Organizing the Campaign

Virtually all the viable state legislative candidates rely on volunteers to perform at least some of the tasks associated with the campaign. In fact, volunteers are a major part of the campaign effort in many states. In Colorado in

1998, the campaign finance laws imposed strict limits on contributions, making it difficult for candidates to generate large sums of money.[11] Even the most aggressive candidates rarely raised more than $25,000, and often they had to get by with considerably less. Under such circumstances, as one successful Colorado candidate told us, "The race at this level depends largely on volunteers."

Sometimes volunteers are supplied by local party organizations. Helping to find and organize volunteers is probably the most important support that the local party organizations can provide. But even this function is not always performed adequately. The strength of the local party organization is highly variable across states and even within a state. Some of the candidates we talked with felt the local party was very helpful; others offered comments such as: "The local party is in disarray," or "The county party organization is virtually nonexistent." And, of course, the local party organization is unlikely to be active in a contested primary, preferring not to choose sides between two or more candidates seeking the party nomination.

Often times the volunteer organization is a product of the candidate's own personal network of friends. This network may be the result of the candidate's previous work on campaigns and local issues, or it may stem from the candidate's active membership in a labor or trade association or other interest group. One successful Alabama candidate (who defeated an incumbent in the primary) relied almost entirely on friends from his church: "We had as many as twelve teams of volunteers working the district. They were mostly members of my church."

Often the volunteer organization is a mix from various networks. As one Democratic candidate running for the state senate in Washington said, "My core group consisted of some party people, some environmentalists, some people from education, some people from labor." Another candidate said her core volunteer group was "a combination of community people and party volunteers."

If the campaign is well funded, the candidate will almost certainly seek some professional help. Less than 15 percent of those candidates with budgets under $50,000 hired advertising or direct mail consultants, while more than half of the candidates with budgets over $50,000 did so.[12] A candidate may hire a media specialist to help produce television and radio ads, and to negotiate the media buys, but more likely he will hire a direct mail expert, if the campaign budget permits. Direct mail is one of the most prevalent ways in which state legislative candidates seek to reach potential voters. As one Alabama candidate said, "I have hired a consulting group out of Birmingham; they charged $3,000 for consulting with a win bonus of $12,000. I do not know what I would have done without them." The consulting group helped the candidate produce four mailings and purchase $6,000 in radio ads the week before the election. He still lost, despite outspending his opponent almost two to one.

The other important position in a campaign is the campaign manager. Many state legislative candidates act as their own campaign manager, but others seek out a friend to serve as manager. A few pay their managers, who usually work for a set fee, often with a negotiated bonus if the candidate wins. The campaign manager oversees the entire campaign operation, and having a manager releases the candidate from spending all his time on the details of the campaign operation. It allows the candidate to spend more time on developing issue positions, getting out in public to meet potential voters, "dialing for dollars," and fundraising in other ways. As Catherine Golden, a former city mayor and veteran of many campaigns notes:

> Of all the tasks in the campaign, asking someone to be the campaign manager is the most difficult. Where other jobs have finite responsibilities and time commitments, the job of campaign manager is open-ended. It is a lot to ask of anyone, especially on a volunteer basis. For this reason, it is usually the first and sometimes the only position to be paid.[13]

Candidates running for seats targeted by the party usually get important organizational and financial help from the state party or the legislative caucus committee (LCC), or sometimes both. Not only do the parties contribute substantial amounts of money to the campaign, but they also assign campaign consultants—usually direct mail experts—to the individual candidates in targeted races.

This often turns out to be a double-edged sword. The candidates had the benefit of professional expertise in conducting the campaign, but several of the candidates felt they were no longer in charge of their own campaign. In fact, one of the candidates we talked with fired the consultant who had been assigned by the LCC, stating, "I didn't like the fact that I had lost some control of the campaign process." Another candidate is convinced she lost in a very tight race because her campaign consultant insisted she send out a "hit piece" on her opponent—a mailer she did not want to send out but was pressured into doing anyway. Of course, the LCC Director had a somewhat different take on the matter: "Some of them [the candidates] think they know what they need to do to win an election, but they don't. We had a few who would have won if they listened."

FUNDRAISING AND ENDORSEMENTS

Most candidates are not in a position to finance their own campaigns, so they must come to grips with the fact that they will have to ask people for money. Unless it is a targeted race (and rarely will the party target more than a dozen or so races in any given election), the candidate can not expect much financial aid from the state party or the LCC. The local (usually county) party can be expected to kick in a few hundred dollars, perhaps. PACs rarely contribute money to challengers, although open seat candidates and those in targeted races may generate significant PAC contributions. Therefore, it usually comes down to asking individuals for money. For the overwhelming majority of candidates, this is by far the most distasteful part of the campaign process. Most candidates express dismay over this task, as this list of comments indicates:

- "I hated the cold calling." (calling people she didn't know and asking them to contribute)
- "I disliked trying to find the money."
- "I hated calling for money."
- "It is futile to run without money, but I know what I have to do to get the money, and I see that as a big drawback. The money aspect is very distasteful. I rebelled at begging for money."
- "I really disliked the fundraising. The amount of money we need to raise and spend offends me personally."
- "Raising money is not my comfort zone."

But the simple, hard fact is that money is an important part of the process, if one wants to be competitive. Especially as a challenger or open-seat candidate, one must have enough money to reach the voters with a message and develop some name recognition. Depending on the state and the nature of the district, one must spend at least $10,000 and often much more. Because of the wide variety of campaign finance laws in different states, fundraising is harder in some states than others. Where contribution limits are low (as they were in Colorado in 1998), one must tap many different donors in order to establish a decent campaign budget.[14]

For nonincumbent candidates, money is raised through three mechanisms: telephone calls, solicitation letters, and events. For most candidates, the most disliked are the telephone calls. Most candidates start with a list of friends and family members. Sometimes the local or state party will provide a list of names and numbers of previous donors. Since the candidate does not personally know most of the people on the "donor list," they find these calls to be particularly awkward. Some of the candidates we interviewed simply refused to "dial for dollars" because they found it embarrassing and demeaning. However, direct contact (face-to-face or by telephone) is considered to be the most effective way to raise money.[15] One candidate in the state of Washington said she spent three hours every day, for several months, making telephone calls soliciting contributions. She raised over $180,000 in a successful bid to unseat the incumbent.

A less intrusive method is the solicitation letter, and is probably the preferred method for most candidates. The candidate sends a letter, often with a campaign flyer enclosed, explaining why she is running, emphasizing her

☑ KATHRYN HAIGH, Democratic candidate for Washington House District 35 seat 1, 1998

Kathryn Haigh is a political party recruiter's dream. She is an energetic, thoughtful, articulate candidate with a history of community involvement. She also happens to be a veterinarian. She and her husband, also a veterinarian, own their own clinic just outside the town of Shelton on the Olympic Peninsula, about twenty-five miles from the state capital of Olympia.

Haigh is a candidate in a very diverse district. The district runs from Bremerton, a naval port, down the peninsula through the farms and old logging communities of Mason County, and ultimately to the suburbs of Olympia, where many state government employees reside.

Like many candidates, Kathy Haigh had been involved in local politics at the school board level, serving on the local school board for twelve years. She knows her way around the legislative halls, having served as the legislative representative for the local school board. Moreover, she is a past president of the Washington State Veterinarian Association and was the legislative contact for the Veterinarians' Political Action Committee.

Haigh was approached by several of the local Democratic precinct committee officers (PCOs), who asked her to run against the incumbent, Peggy Johnson. Johnson is a conservative Republican and chair of the House Education Committee. Haigh's school board experience meant she was well aware of Peggy Johnson's education policies, many of which Kathy Haigh strongly disagreed with.

Haigh made the decision to run by mid-January of 1998. She formally announced her candidacy in March. While the local party organization helped get out volunteers for the campaign, it did not provide much money. She did, however, receive substantial financial backing and campaign help from the House Democratic Campaign Committee. And the contacts she made as president of the Veterinarian Association turned out to be surprisingly helpful; she received campaign contributions from veterinarians both in-state and out-of-state. "I had no idea how many individuals would give money," she commented.

Because of the size of the legislative districts in Washington (about 90,000 people per district), and because hers was a targeted, very competitive race in which party control of the house chamber was potentially at stake, the campaign was intense and expensive. Kathy Haigh raised and spent $85,000 (her opponent spent $106,000). The House Democratic Caucus hired a campaign consultant to work with her. The consultant handled a lot of the work on the six mailings Haigh sent out, but she found working with a consultant to be difficult. On the one hand, it took some of the day-to-day work burden off her, but at the same time she felt she "lost some control over the process at that point."

When asked about the campaign experience, she said, "What I learned was that it takes the same sort of commitment that vet school took—just not for as long." She started campaigning full time on June 15. Driving up and down the district, she put eighteen thousand miles on her automobile in less than five months. She even did some of the canvassing on her bicycle. She found the doorbelling "hard at first, but it got easier. Once people knew who I was, it was really fun." The campaign was long and arduous. "I can't remember anything from those five months. There is the feeling you should always be doing something else, something more. I discovered Tylenol PM or would never have been able to sleep, worrying about what else I should be doing." In terms of the effect on her family (husband and two teenage sons) she said, "You just aren't there physically or emotionally during the campaign process. My husband didn't realize how much the campaign would invade the home space—the telephone ringing constantly, etcetera."

Kathryn Haigh won the election, defeating the incumbent 51 to 49 percent.

campaign theme, and closing with a request for money. A return envelope is included. Some candidates hold small events such as coffees, luncheons, or parties to raise money. One candidate in Colorado held ten such events.

Besides money, candidates also seek endorsements. In particular, they seek endorsements from well-known individuals in the community and from interest groups and organizations. Both types of endorsements are important because they lend legitimacy to the individual's campaign. They often lead to more money and volunteers as well; this is especially true of interest-group endorsements.

Candidates also hope for endorsements from the newspaper editorial boards in their community. Although candidates are quick to point out that, "I received the *Daily Chronicle*'s endorsement," it is unclear how much such newspaper endorsements really help the cause. However, candidates believe that such endorsements lend legitimacy to their campaign.

The newspaper editorial boards and many interest groups often invite the various candidates to an interview session before deciding whom to endorse. These sessions usually last about an hour and give the board members an opportunity to ask the candidates about their stands on various issues and to assess the candidates' qualifications. Some candidates enjoy these sessions, finding them to be interesting and energizing. Others said they disliked these meetings intensely, especially if one or more opponents were in the room at the same time.

Increasingly, interest groups and even some newspaper boards bypass the interview session in favor of sending a questionnaire that seeks information about the candidate's position on issues important to the group. Many candidates said that one of the most surprising things about the campaign process was the number of surveys and questionnaires they received. Some candidates claimed to have received as many as sixty or seventy surveys.

CONTACTING THE VOTERS

State legislative campaigns tend to be "intimate and retail," meaning they use face-to-face methods of voter contact.[16] "Wholesale" techniques, such as advertising on television or even radio, are not particularly prevalent because of the cost. Instead, candidates often rely on billboards and yard signs, which are low-cost forms of mass advertising. The only other "mass" technique generally used is direct mail, but this is usually targeted to specific segments of the voting population.

State legislative campaigns need to contact the voters in effective and cost-efficient ways. They use direct mail; they go to places where they are likely to find lots of people, such as candidate forums, county fairs, local sporting events, shopping centers, and Fourth of July parades; and they go door-to-door, doing "literature drops" and talking to people one-on-one. In some New

England states, candidates even campaign at the town dump and recycling center on Saturdays, when many people are disposing of their trash or dropping off their bottles and plastics! The relative mix of techniques will depend on the nature of the district, the size of the campaign budget, the volunteer organization, and the candidate's own abilities and preferences.

CANDIDATE FORUMS

Most candidates feel obliged to attend these candidate forums sponsored by groups such as the local Chamber of Commerce or the League of Women Voters. Most forums are held after the primary election, when the field of candidates is narrowed down. One advantage to participating in these meetings is that sometimes the local media covers them. State legislative candidates look for any free media coverage they can get.

Many candidates believe forums are a useful way to get some name recognition and lend legitimacy to the campaign. Others disagree, arguing that when one tallies up the time required to drive to the forum, sit through all the other candidates' stump speeches, answer questions, mingle afterwards, and then drive back home, an entire evening is gone. One successful Colorado candidate said, "I listened to the people who said 'hit direct mail, and don't waste time going to candidate forums.'" In his case, this strategy worked.

One of the oldest campaign techniques is to "go where the people are." Candidates shake hands and pass out literature at the shopping malls or at the Friday night high school football games. One Colorado candidate said his favorite campaign technique was to stand in front of the entrance to the local supermarket, greeting customers and handing out campaign brochures. A candidate can be seen by, shake hands with, and briefly talk to hundreds of people in a couple of hours. Of course, there is no guarantee that all those people live in the district or that they vote. One certain advantage to this technique is that it is inexpensive. The only costs are the candidate's time and the price for printing the campaign flyers or brochures that are handed out to passers-by.

DIRECT MAIL

One of the consequences of the computer age is that it is relatively easy to devise targeted mailing lists that can be used to deliver a tailored message on different issues to different groups. In most races, direct mail is too expensive to use until after the primary election. But in states with primaries as late as August or September, or where the electoral laws call for open or blanket primaries, direct mail may be used in primary contests. In the state of Washington, which has a September blanket primary, some candidates produced as many as three different mailings prior to the primary. One Republican candidate in Colorado reported that he sent out over seven thousand postcards to registered Republicans before the primary.

Most successful candidates use direct mail to contact the voters. The total cost of each mailing depends on the number of households in the district, but in most states it amounts to several thousand dollars. In the state of Washington, for example, a typical mailing costs between $8,000 and $10,000. In Idaho, where the legislative districts are much smaller, the average cost is $2,000 to $3,000.

Targeted mailings are sent to a subset of the district voters who are the most likely to vote, which is determined from voting lists indicating how often an individual has voted in previous elections. Each mailing focuses on a specific issue, such as health care, and is targeted to a specific audience, like senior citizens. While the overall mailing costs will be lower (since not all households are targeted), the production costs are greater because several different brochures or cards must be created. Because of tight budgets, most candidates can not afford to make more than two or three direct mailings. Some make none at all. But one well-funded challenger managed ten separate mailings in a span of seven weeks. Since direct mail has become an important and relatively sophisticated component of many state legislative campaigns, those who can afford to will usually hire a professional to help them.

WALKING THE DISTRICT

Perhaps the most effective way to reach the voters is to walk from house to house, meeting potential voters face to face. It is, however, also the most time consuming and physically demanding way. It requires remarkable stamina and tremendous will to spend three to four hours every day canvassing the various neighborhoods. It may take months. One candidate in Washington said he "doorbelled" 16,300 houses. At least four others said they rang 12,000 to 13,000 doorbells. One candidate, whose district was semi-rural, rode her bicycle from house to house. Most of these candidates won. But it is physically exhausting work.

Going door-to-door is the activity that most candidates, to their own surprise, find they truly enjoyed. One candidate, a college professor, told us, "Meeting people outside of academia was fun. I met a couple of thousand people I would not have met otherwise." Others made similar comments:

- "I found I really enjoyed the house-to-house thing, and I was dreading it the most."
- "I really liked the doorbelling; people want to be engaged; they want to talk."
- "I found doorbelling really enjoyable. It was hard at first, but it got easier. Once people knew who I was, it was really fun."
- "I really liked meeting people. I met a lot of people who were genuinely concerned about the issues."

Even the nature of door-to-door campaigning can vary by the type of district. In highly urban areas, many of the potential voters live in condominiums or apartments with security guards or gates, making it difficult for the candidate to gain access. Also, in some neighborhoods, many people are not home during the day so doorbelling can only be done in the early evenings or on the weekends.

CANDIDATES' PERCEPTIONS OF THEIR CAMPAIGN ABILITIES

Those who make the commitment to run tend to have a fairly high assessment of their own abilities to organize and conduct a campaign. The overwhelming majority of candidates are optimistic about their ability to run a campaign; over 90 percent rated their ability as "fair" or "high"; over 50 percent said "high" (see Table 4.1). An even higher percentage of candidates felt they had "fair" or "high" skills as public speakers. Most candidates seemed to feel they had decent support from the political party, especially the local or district party. They were less sanguine about their abilities to raise campaign funds.

Not surprisingly, candidates who had already held an elective office were generally more sure of their abilities than those without experience (see Table 4.2 on page 90). They were more than twice as likely to say that their name recognition in the district was high, and they were more likely to rate themselves higher in terms of their ability to run a campaign, garner support from both the local and state parties, and raise money.

TABLE 4.1   CANDIDATES' SELF-PERCEPTIONS OF CAMPAIGN ABILITIES

HOW WOULD YOU RATE YOURSELF ON THE FOLLOWING?	LOW	FAIR	HIGH	NOT SURE
Name recognition (N = 530)	20.4%	48.0%	29.2%	1.3%
Ability to run a campaign (N = 529)	7.8	39.5	50.9	1.7
Public speaking ability (N = 531)	6.2	40.5	53.3	0.0
Support from your party in the district (N = 528)	20.1	32.6	45.6	1.7
Support from your own state party (N = 521)	27.4	30.1	37.4	5.0
Local fundraising ability (N = 529)	23.1	46.9	26.3	3.8
PAC fundraising ability (N = 510)	33.7	36.3	18.8	11.2
Ability to fund own campaign (N = 526)	53.2	26.2	19.2	1.0

Note: The number of respondents varies slightly from one item to another, due to missing answers.
Source: The Legislative Candidate Survey

TABLE 4.2 PERCENTAGE OF CANDIDATES RATING
THEIR ABILITIES "HIGH," BY ELECTIVE EXPERIENCE

ABILITIES	NOT CURRENTLY IN ELECTIVE OFFICE	CURRENTLY IN ELECTIVE OFFICE
Name recognition in the district	23.4%	47.0%
Ability to run a campaign	49.6	54.2
Public speaking ability	54.8	49.2
Support from your party in the district	43.9	50.4
Support from your own state party	34.9	44.6
Local fundraising ability	23.7	34.1
PAC fundraising ability	16.7	25.6
Ability to fund own campaign	18.8	20.5

Source: The Legislative Candidate Survey

CONCLUSION

Except in a few states like California, state legislative races are not conducted in the same way as congressional campaigns. State legislative candidates deliver their campaign messages on the doorstep and through the mailbox. Campaign brochures and yard signs tend to be more prevalent than television ads. In most places, state legislative candidates engage in "retail" rather than "wholesale" politics.

The American public does not recognize, and therefore does not appreciate, the personal efforts that state legislative candidates make. Many of the candidates themselves underestimated the effort that would be required to run a serious campaign. They often made statements such as, "I had no idea what I was getting myself into," or "This was a lot harder than I expected." In part, these candidates were talking about the sheer physical effort of campaigning.

One of the most difficult aspects of the campaign process is its potential effect on the candidate's family. The campaign intrudes on the household and is a tremendous distraction from the normal family interactions. As one candidate in a high profile state senate race said, "You shouldn't ever do this [run for office] unless you have a passion for it. You shouldn't put your family through it unless you are absolutely driven."

But perhaps the most difficult part of candidacy is the emotional risk. Candidates suffer anxiety, frustration, and fatigue. At one point in a tough campaign in the state of Washington, a candidate told her husband, "I hate this. Don't ever let me do this again." Another female candidate summed it up this way: "You get tired of people yelling obscene things at you, calling you a bitch, flipping you off." It is, perhaps, this personal aspect of candidacy that the general public least understands or appreciates. Candidates are pretty much ordinary people with a sense of civic responsibility, a keen interest in politics, or a particular issue that motivates them.

In the end, after all the physical work, the distasteful fundraising, and the emotional ups and downs, most candidates, win or lose, found the campaign experience to be a good one in which they learned a lot about themselves and about the process. Dave Custer was one such candidate. He ran as the Republican candidate for the Colorado Senate in 1998. A former high school math teacher and engineer for Bell Laboratories in the Denver area, this was his first attempt at public office. After losing his bid for a seat in the Colorado senate, Dave wrote down his reflections on running a campaign. He provides excellent advice for anyone considering a state legislative race.

THINGS TO DO DIFFERENTLY

BY DAVE CUSTER

The following are some thoughts I want to offer to you. The campaign was a tremendous learning experience for me. I did a lot of things right. And I made a lot of mistakes. I hope you can benefit from my experience.

1. Don't dutifully answer questionnaires without *qualifying your answer* and referring to a position paper for full details. Entice the newspaper reporter or PAC to read and understand your position fully. Try to get in-person interviews even if you have to travel.

2. *Examine your issues and prioritize them.* Before deciding on a no-compromise campaign, look at several questions. Would you rather not be elected than not soften your position on an issue? I should have softened my position on vouchers; I should have honored the repeated citizen rejection of tax relief for parents of non-public school children. It was not worth losing lots of votes and possibly a major newspaper endorsement. And perhaps even the election. Sometimes it is hard to remember that it is an imperfect world and we just have to do the best we can under the circumstances.

3. *Don't write off any newspaper.* Remember newspapers buy their ink by the barrel! Look and see what previous endorsements have been given. Make sure you send your position papers that will reinforce your qualifications in the areas of interest to them.

4. *Walking the district* is the most valuable thing you can do, and the most expensive in terms of your time. Start during the primary season. Make a plan. How many doors in the district do you need to

knock on? Which ones? How many each week? How many each
day? Which days are you going to walk? Which hours? Make a cal-
endar. Post the numbers and a chart showing your progress. Put it
where you have to look at it several times a day and feel guilty if
you aren't keeping to your schedule. Getting started is the hardest.
After a while I found I was enjoying walking the district. I wish I
had been able to do more. Have someone go with you. You walk
one side of the street; they walk the other.

5. *Try to find a catch phrase* that describes what you want to do on an
issue. I didn't invent "restore the checks and balances in the educational system" until late in the campaign. I am convinced that phrase,
along with a position paper, would have made a difference. It would
have made me stand out, worthy of some attention. How many
politicians talk about fixing the public school system? How many
have a plan? You want to be the one with the plan.

6. *Write a position paper* for each of your major issues. Without a position paper all you have is hand waving. Reporters will respect you
more for it. Position papers will distinguish you from the general
run-of-the-mill candidate. A position paper will save you much time
in the long run. A position paper will help guide a discussion in the
direction you want it to go. Write a position paper for all your major
issues *before the primary season starts!!!*

7. *Tell all your friends, relatives, and co-workers* that you are running for
office. They will all be interested. Even if your company has rules
against solicitation, tell your co-workers; a simple statement of fact
is not a solicitation. Ask if it is OK to call in the evening or week-
end. Be sure to ask for their support if you do get permission to call.
Ask even if it causes you extreme embarrassment. I found it easier
to ask by mail than in person. But I think in person is more effective. You pay for what you get. No pain, no gain. There is no free
lunch. Sigh.

8. I have come to believe that *anything positive you do* will increase your
percentage of the vote. If you have the necessary budget, do them all,
even if you find some of them personally objectionable. I personally don't like bulk mail and I resent computerized phone calls. But if
I had the budget, I would do both.

9. *Color sells.* Consider using full color in your literature. Use a picture
of yourself on every piece of literature you can.

10. The American voter seems to prefer *the candidate closest to the center.*
Can you move to the center in good conscience? If you can, do so.
Use this test on each issue.

11. *Find a real blunt SOB* to serve on your committee. Someone who will
let you have it with both barrels when you screw up. And you will.

You must learn from your mistakes, just don't keep repeating them. Don't feel too bad about the first time you make a mistake. The tenth time you make the same mistake, you should feel real bad about it.

12. *Always have the outline of a speech* in your pocket. Never mind that you have said the same thing two hundred times, and the last time was just five minutes ago. If your audience has never heard it before, it will be fresh and new to them. My biggest embarrassment of the campaign came because I thought I could wing it. If you try to wing it, you might end up looking like an idiot, as I did, and convince much of your audience that they really don't want to vote for you.

13. In private have someone *videotape your canned speech.* Watch the videotape. Make changes. Repeat this procedure until it is OK. Now try it in front of an audience of supporters. Make any necessary changes. Videotape the modified speech three times. Repeat until everything is satisfactory or until none of your supporters will watch it again, whichever comes first!

14. When you speak in public, try to have one of your supporters *watch the audience,* not you. Have them note what works and what doesn't. If something consistently doesn't work, modify it or remove it. Sometimes things change during a campaign. Watch for these changes. But don't change your position without lots of thought.

15. *Be prepared to work harder* than you ever had to before. I never used to believe politicians when they talked about how much work a campaign was. I do now.

Notes

1. There are many accounts of the reasons for this decline, but for a good brief summary, see John Bibby, "State and Local Parties in a Candidate-Centered Age," in *American State and Local Politics,* ed. Ronald Weber and Paul Brace (New York: Chatham House Publishers, 1999), 196–198.

2. See Stephen Salmore and Barbara Salmore, "The Transformation of State Electoral Politics," in *The State of States,* 3rd ed., ed. Carl E. Van Horn (Washington, D.C.: CQ Press, 1996), 51–76.

3. State senate districts are larger, of course. Half the states have state senate districts with populations of 100,000 or more. Texas senate districts each contain close to 600,000 people, and California senate districts average about 800,000 inhabitants. Thus, in those two states, legislative districts are similar in size to congressional districts.

4. For those who want more precise numbers: after the next redistricting cycle in 2001 and 2002, there will be approximately 1031 state senators and about 800 state

representatives with 100,000 or more people in their districts. This represents about 52 percent of all state senate districts and about 15 percent of all house districts.

5. Anthony Gierzynski, "Elections to the State Legislature," in *Encyclopedia of the American Legislative System*, ed. Joel H. Silbey (New York: Charles Scribner & Sons, 1994), 441.

6. Paul Herrnson, *Congressional Elections*, 2nd ed. (Washington, D.C.: CQ Press, 1998), 182.

7. Robert E. Hogan, "Voter Contact Techniques in State Legislative Campaigns," *Legislative Studies Quarterly* 22 (1997): 560.

8. For a good discussion of the role of media in politics, see Stephen Ansolabehere, Roy Behr, and Shanto Iyengar, *The Media Game: American Politics in the Television Age* (New York: Macmillan Publishing Co., 1993).

9. One study of state legislative candidates in the 1998 election found that, among candidates who spent less than $50,000 on their campaign, only 13 percent purchased broadcast television time and 19 percent bought time on cable TV. Candidates who spent more than $50,000 were more likely to purchase broadcast (38 percent) and cable (45 percent) time. See Ron Faucheux and Paul Herrnson, "See How They Run: State Legislative Candidates," *Campaigns & Elections* (August 1999): 25.

10. One recent study that investigated campaigns for the lower houses of state legislatures in 1994 found that the average spending by candidates (including incumbents) exceeded $50,000 in only three of the fourteen states examined. See Gary F. Moncrief, "Candidate Spending in State Legislative Races," in *Campaign Finance in State Legislative Elections*, ed. Joel Thompson and Gary F. Moncrief (Washington, D.C.: CQ Press, 1998).

11. The law has since been declared unconstitutional, and as of this writing there are now no limits on campaign contributions in Colorado.

12. Faucheux and Herrnson, "See How They Run," 25.

13. Catherine M. Golden, *The Campaign Manager* (Ashland, Oreg.: Oak Street Press, 1996), 17.

14. One of our most vivid recollections while interviewing candidates in Colorado is sitting at one particular candidate's kitchen table, attempting to talk to him about the campaign experience while he carefully opened envelope after envelope, peering in to see if they contained checks from donors. Each time he found a check inside, he would carefully extract it and hand it to his wife (who served as his treasurer) with a comment: "Fred came through, honey" or "I was hoping for more from them." Clearly, he was far more interested in the checks than in our interview.

15. Golden, *The Campaign Manager*, 56.

16. Ronald Keith Gaddie, "'The Hopes That Lie in the Hearts of Young Men' Part 1: The Origins of Political Ambition" (Paper presented at the Annual Meeting of the Southwestern Political Science Association, San Antonio, Tex., March 1998), 11.

5

THE ROAD LESS TRAVELED:
WOMEN, MINORITY,
AND THIRD-PARTY CANDIDATES

State legislatures have always been bastions of middle-aged, white males. But over the last decade, more women and minorities have been elected. In this chapter, we look at the recruitment patterns that bring women and minorities to run for the legislature. We also look at another group that is still rarely found in American state legislatures: third-party members. Virtually all state legislators are elected as Republicans or Democrats; less than 1 percent of state legislators represent some other party. In many states, however, third-party candidates for the state legislature are becoming more common, and in some districts they are the only alternative to the incumbent on the ballot.

The number of women serving in the state legislature varies considerably across the states. The Washington state legislature has a higher percentage of women, 41 percent, serving in the year 2000 than any other state legislature. At the other end of the scale, only 8 percent of Alabama legislators in 2000 are women, the lowest percentage of women legislators of all the states.

The difference between these two states is dramatic, and it begins at the recruitment stage. Only 12 percent of the candidates running in the primary election for the Alabama legislature were women (see Table 5.1 on page 96), while almost 30 percent of the state legislative candidates in the Washington primary were female. The likelihood that a candidate in the primary election was a woman was almost three times greater in Washington than in Alabama. This disparity also shows up in the general election, where over 31 percent of the contestants were women in Washington compared to only 11 percent in Alabama.

TABLE 5.1   THE FATE OF FEMALE CANDIDATES IN ALABAMA
AND WASHINGTON IN THE 1998 ELECTIONS

	ALABAMA			WASHINGTON		
	TOTAL CANDIDATES	FEMALE	% FEMALE	TOTAL CANDIDATES	FEMALE	% FEMALE
Primary Election	339	39	12%	264	77	30%
General Election	227	26	11	209	65	31
Elected	140	11	8	122	48	39
Percent of women entering the primary who were elected to the legislature		28				62

Note: The table includes both house and senate candidates. In Alabama, all lower and upper house seats were up for election in 1998, while in Washington all lower house and one-half of the senate seats were up for election. All figures in the table are calculated by the authors.

Moreover, women candidates in Washington were very successful; 62 percent of all female candidates who entered the primary in Washington ultimately were elected to the state legislature. In Alabama, only 28 percent of the women candidates who entered primaries ended up being elected to the legislature. And remember that far more women ran in Washington than in Alabama. While the figures from these two states represent the extreme cases, they do point out that the opportunity structure, the political culture, and the success rate for women candidates are quite different in different states.

DEMOGRAPHIC AND ECONOMIC DIFFERENCES BETWEEN MEN AND WOMEN CANDIDATES

Demographically, there are few dramatic differences between men and women candidates for the state legislature. Candidate age is one of these. Almost 75 percent of women candidates are in their forties or fifties, while only 55 percent of men are in that age bracket. More men run at younger and older ages than do women, probably because women postpone running for political office while their children are young.[1]

Education levels are virtually the same between the men and women in our survey. Most have at least attended college, and over half have a college degree or postgraduate degree. Candidates for the state legislature are overwhelmingly white, regardless of sex.

A greater percentage of women candidates are either divorced or separated from their spouses than are men candidates, and women candidates are also more likely to be widowed.[2] Apparently, more women than men are comfortable running for office without the support of a spouse.

Almost the same percentages of men and women candidates have children living at home. But almost no women under the age of thirty who have children at home run for office, while some men of the same age who also have children do run.[3] Having younger children at home appears to constrain potential women candidates in a way that older children do not.

**DIFFERENCES IN THE POLITICAL CONTEXT
OF RUNNING FOR THE LEGISLATURE**

One of the questions about the prospects for women running for office is whether women are more likely than men to be recruited as "sacrificial lambs" in long-shot races.[4] In the 1997–1998 electoral cycle, men were actually slightly more likely to make the more difficult race against an incumbent than were women (see Table 5.2). Concomitantly, women were slightly more likely than men to be found in open-seat races where the chances for victory were better.

The decision to plunge into a state legislative race is one that is made on a relatively tight deadline for candidates of both sexes. The filing deadline varies from state to state, but it usually occurs about two to three months before the primary election. Women candidates are a bit more apt to enter the race within five months of the primary. On the other end of the scale, a higher proportion of men than women made the decision to enter the race at least a year before the primary. Women seem to be more contemplative in their decision and less apt to leap early into a race before carefully assessing the situation.

What political backgrounds do men and women candidates bring to the campaign? While few state legislative candidates have run for political office before, for the most part they are not political neophytes (see Table 5.3 on page 98). Most candidates have some political experience working on campaigns

TABLE 5.2   TYPE OF RACE AND TIMING OF DECISION TO ENTER

	MEN (N = 418)	WOMEN (N = 115)
TYPE OF RACE		
General election challenger	50%	47%
Primary election challenger	7	8
Open seat	43	45
WHEN CANDIDATE DECIDED TO ENTER RACE	*(N = 419)*	*(N = 115)*
Within the last 2 months	27%	32%
3–5 months before primary	28	31
6–12 months before primary	24	23
More than a year before primary	21	14

Source: Legislative Candidate Survey

TABLE 5.3   POLITICAL EXPERIENCE LEVEL
OF MALE AND FEMALE MAJOR-PARTY CANDIDATES

TYPE OF POLITICAL EXPERIENCE	MEN (N = 420)	WOMEN (N = 116)
Active or Very Active in:		
Federal Campaign	64%	59%
Statewide Campaign	65	69
Local Campaign	72	78
Held:		
Some Party Post	61	59
More than One Post	30	33
Currently Hold:		
Appointive Office	10	8
Elective Office	23	29
Seeking Lower House Seat	22	23
Seeking Upper House Seat	28	48
Ran for Legislature Before:		
In Primary Only	9	2
In General Election	16	17
Served on:		
State Legislative Staff	4	6
Congressional Staff	3	3
Both Staffs	1	2

Source: Legislative Candidate Survey

or holding a position in the party. Moreover, women candidates have slightly more political experience than do their male counterparts. The extensive background Jeanne Edwards, a Washington state Democrat, brought to her 1998 race for a house seat is not unusual. She served on the Bothell city council for seven years, was a former chair of the Washington Board of Transportation, had worked as a legislative staff member, and had covered the state legislature as a journalist.

Or consider the political resume presented by Nancy Spence, a Republican candidate for the Colorado House in 1998. She had been a member of her local school board for three terms in the 1980s and early 1990s, and had served as the president of a Parent Teacher Organization. She also had been very active in party politics, managing campaigns for several GOP candidates and serving as a delegate to a National Republican Convention.

Indeed, the substantially higher percentage of women currently holding elective office who are running for a seat in the state senate suggests that women are particularly strategic in their decision making about if and when to run for higher office. The women who choose to run for the state legislature are not apt to be naive about the difficulties of running for office; they have been involved in politics in a number of different ways before they make the race.

THE SOCIAL CONTEXT OF DECIDING TO RUN

Are women state legislative candidates recruited to run or are they self-starters? Women report more recruitment contacts than do men (see Table 5.4). Women candidates are more apt to get encouragement from state party officials, local elected officials, and legislative leaders.[5] Women also report more recruitment efforts from nonparty sources, particularly from service organizations. The local Chamber of Commerce, for example, encouraged Lynda Straub to run for the Alabama House in 1998 (see Candidate Profile on pages 100–101).

Men are more likely to be self-starters than are women candidates. Over a third of the male candidates agreed with the statement, "It was entirely my idea to run," while only 11 percent of women candidates did (see Table 5.5 on page 102). These were the people who were ready to run even without encouragement, the candidates we would consider to be self-starters. Roughly half of male and female candidates said, "I had already thought of running when someone else encouraged me to run." These are the candidates who may have been leaning toward running when someone urged them to do so. Only 18 percent of men claimed, "I had not seriously thought about running until someone else suggested it to me," but 37 percent of women agreed with that statement. Despite having very similar levels of political experience, far fewer women were apt to jump into the race on their own initiative. This is consistent with the observations of a female political activist in Iowa, who noted during a rally to encourage women to run for office that, "Sometimes I think women need to be asked to run for office.... They need that extra push."[6]

TABLE 5.4   DIFFERENCES BETWEEN MEN AND WOMEN
IN RECRUITMENT CONTACTS (MAJOR-PARTY CANDIDATES)

	MEN ($N = 420$)	WOMEN ($N = 116$)
PARTY ENCOURAGEMENT TO RUN		
Local Party Officials	46%	47%
State Party Officials*	31	42
Local Elected Officials*	31	44
Legislative Leaders*	31	42
NONPARTY ENCOURAGEMENT TO RUN		
Church Members	12%	12%
Neighbors	21	28
Interest Groups	12	18
Co-workers	18	24
Service Organizations*	15	28

*Difference is statistically significant at .05 or better.
Source: Legislative Candidate Survey

☑ LYNDA STRAUB, Democratic candidate for the Alabama House District 105, 1998

Lynda Straub is a successful businesswoman who ran against one-term incumbent Phil Crigler. This particular contest promised to be one of the most expensive and competitive house races in Alabama. Crigler is a congenial, low-key conservative with strong support from the Christian Coalition. In 1994, he challenged and upset a powerful, long-time Democratic incumbent.

Straub lives in a small community southwest of Mobile, just a few miles from the Gulf of Mexico. She has been active in community affairs, helping to organize Citizens for A Better Grand Bay, a local organization intent on cleaning up the town and obtaining funds for a community center. Because she owns several local stores, including a florist shop and a pharmacy, she has long been involved in the Bayou La Batre Area Chamber of Commerce. Indeed, it was some of her Chamber associates who essentially "drafted" her by urging her to enter the race, then telling others in the community that she was going to run before she had actually decided to. In the beginning, she was reluctant to run.

"At first I thought, 'I'm not qualified.' But after visiting Montgomery [the state capital], I said, 'If these bozos can do this, I know I can do it.'" The timing was good because her children were grown and out of the house, and she had the support of some influential Democrats. She ultimately decided to run because of frustration over the lack of funding for the community center and her discovery that there were so few women in the Alabama legislature. Once she opted to make the race, she devoted tremendous energy and money to the effort. She hired a campaign manager and spent about $60,000 on the race. She produced at least five mailings, each one devoted to a different issue. While she received financial support from individual contributors and the party, she also invested a considerable amount of her own money in the campaign.

Because she is an intelligent, dynamic, and successful local merchant, Lynda Straub was an attractive candidate—even as a challenger running against a popular incumbent. But the fact of the matter is, it is still difficult for a woman to get elected to the state legislature in Alabama. Only 8 percent of the state's legislators are female—the lowest percentage in the nation. Concerned by this state of affairs, a nonpartisan group called Alabama Solutions formed in 1990 to provide seed money to female candidates. This group contributed $1,000 to Lynda

Straub's campaign. One of the founders of Alabama Solutions, Natalie Davis (a political science professor at Birmingham Southern College), thinks that the group is going to have to do more than provide seed money: "We are going to have to become more active in actually recruiting women candidates."

Meanwhile, Lynda Straub maintains her sense of humor about the situation. When asked why she decided to run, she jokingly says, "I had a Prozac moment."

Lynda Straub lost to incumbent Phil Crigler, 44 to 56 percent.

LYNDA STRAUB

★ CARING
★ DEDICATED
★ ENERGETIC
★ DETERMINED
★ BUSINESSWOMAN
★ COMMUNITY
   LEADER

The Lynda Straub material is reprinted with the permission of Lynda Straub.

TABLE 5.5   DIFFERENCES IN RESPONSE TO "WHOSE IDEA WAS IT
TO RUN FOR LEGISLATURE?" (MAJOR-PARTY CANDIDATES)

SOURCE OF IDEA TO RUN FOR THE STATE LEGISLATURE*	MEN (N = 366)	WOMEN (N = 98)
"It was entirely my idea."	37%	11%
"I had already thought about it when someone else encouraged me to run."	45	52
"I had not seriously thought about it until someone else suggested it."	18	37

*Differences are statistically significant at better than .01.
Source: Legislative Candidate Survey
Note: In New Jersey, the question was posed slightly differently and respondents from that state are not included in this table. The response options in New Jersey were: "It was entirely my idea" and "I had not seriously thought about running until someone else suggested it." Of 52 male respondents, 71 percent said it was entirely their idea to run, while only 35 percent of the 17 female respondents said the same. Conversely, only 29 percent of the male respondents indicated they had not seriously thought about running until someone else suggested it; 65 percent of the women opted for this response.

POLITICAL PARTY EFFORTS TO RECRUIT WOMEN AS CANDIDATES

If women need an extra push to run for office, to what extent are those who are recruiting legislative candidates willing to provide one? Is it easier or harder for them to recruit female candidates? There are lessons on this score to be learned from the Democrats' experiences in Vermont over the last two decades. Between the 1984 and 1998 sessions of the Vermont legislature, the number of female Democratic senators increased from three to ten, and the number of female Republican senators doubled, from one to two. The number of female Democratic representatives jumped from fifteen to thirty-four, and the number of female Republican representatives rose just slightly to fourteen from thirteen. These outcomes occurred partly because more Democrats were being elected to the Vermont legislature during this time period, but also because the Democrats were running more women as candidates.

During the 1983–1984 session, Ralph Wright, the Democratic minority leader in the Vermont House, launched a vigorous and sustained effort to recruit more and better Democratic candidates to run for house seats. Over a period of several elections, he was able to narrow the gap between the parties enough to be elected speaker with a few Republican votes. He finally led the Democrats to a solid majority in the 1992 election. From the start, Wright made a serious effort to recruit women as candidates. He noted the following:

> We recruited women. We didn't set out to do it, but it wasn't long before we realized there was a big political difference between the sexes.... Simply stated, women make better candidates than men. One reason was political, the other philosophic. They were candidates uncorrupted by the process.[7]

After Wright left the legislature following the 1994 election, his succes-
sors continued to actively recruit women candidates. Between the 1984 session
and the 1998 session, the number of Democratic representatives increased by
23 (from 65 to 88)—an increase almost totally accounted for by female Democrats, who increased by 19 (from 15 to 34).

When Joanne Davidson became a GOP leader in the Ohio House of Representatives, she discovered for herself what a tough job it was to recruit
women to run for office. She learned, "Women are a harder sell because they
are more realistic about what their chances are and what you are going to do
for them. They ask tougher questions. They are less likely to be risk takers because they have less confidence in themselves." Davidson noted, however,
that the dearth of women candidates was not simply because they were reluctant to run. She also complained, "In some counties the local party leaders
don't believe a woman can carry their district, which hurts the recruiting effort." In those districts, leaders were unwilling to provide potential women
candidates the necessary push to get them into the race.

Despite working hard, Davidson had been no more successful than her
predecessors in recruiting women. From 1983 through 1992, the Republicans
had only three or four women in the house. But this was a period when the
party was mired in the minority, failing to make any consistent gains and
stuck at no more than 40 percent of the seats, a situation that made it hard to
get more women elected to the legislature. In the 1992 election, the Republicans gained eight seats, six more Republican women were elected, and Davidson became minority leader. The Republicans gained ten more seats in the
1994 election, giving them a solid majority, and Davidson was chosen speaker of the house. By the 1997–1998 session, there were fourteen Republican
women in the house. It would appear that the growth in the number of Republican seats gave Republican women a better chance of being elected, and
Joanne Davidson's rise to minority leader and then speaker presumably
meant that the top party leadership was more strongly committed to recruiting women.

In several states, women holding legislative leadership positions have
been given much of the responsibility for recruiting women as candidates.
Mary Webster, the Republican minority leader in the Maine House in
1989–1990, worked hard on recruiting candidates, including women. She
found it hard to recruit women, partly because younger women often had responsibility for children and were very reluctant to run unless they lived close
enough to the capital city so that they could commute every day. She had first-
hand knowledge of the problem; when she was first elected to the legislature,
she had children aged two, four, six, and eight.

A Republican female legislator in North Carolina who had been in leadership in the late 1980s concurred that it was harder to recruit those women
who had heavy family responsibilities. But she said that, in general, it was
hard to get any Republicans to run because, at that time, they were still very

much a minority party. She also felt that it was no harder to recruit women than men, and that, as a woman, she could be more persuasive than a male recruiter.

Most of the states with the lowest proportion of women in the legislature are southern or border states. Natalie Davis, a political science professor and a former candidate for statewide office in Alabama, is a founding member of an organization that helps to fund women candidates for statewide and legislative office. This organization provides female candidates with seed money that they can use to set up their campaigns and to raise other funds. Davis thinks that women who are potential candidates are handicapped because they are "not wired to the interest groups," which for Alabama Democrats means they lack support from organizations representing teachers groups, trial lawyers, and often African-Americans. Davis believes her group has to start targeting districts and recruiting women in a state where the Democratic party does little or no systematic recruiting.

CANDIDATE SELF-PERCEPTIONS ABOUT THEIR CANDIDACIES

Do men and women candidates assess their candidacies differently? On some dimensions, men and women have the same evaluations of themselves as candidates. Men and women candidates, for example, give themselves virtually the same marks for name recognition in their districts and for the ability to finance their campaigns out of their own pockets (see Table 5.6).

Women candidates, however, expressed more confidence in their ability to organize and run their campaigns and in their speaking abilities than did men candidates, perhaps because many of the women who opt to run are those with campaign experience. Their background in politics may help breed confidence in their abilities to run their own campaigns and to speak before the public. Women candidates also report receiving more support from their local party and from the state party than do men candidates.[8] The considerable assistance Fran Coleman received when she ran for the Colorado House is consistent with this perception (see the Candidate Profile on pages 106–107).

TERM LIMITS AND THE RECRUITMENT OF WOMEN CANDIDATES

When term limits first passed in the early 1990s, there was much speculation about what they would mean for the prospects of electing more women to state legislatures. Yet the evidence suggests that, so far, term limits have made little difference on this score.[9] The 1998 election results in Michigan are a good example: Term limits in that state went into effect for the first time that year, but women held the same number of seats after the election as before it. Following the election, a female former Michigan legislator lamented that while sixteen newly elected women "gained an opportunity, sixteen women lost an opportunity [by being forced out]," adding that "there's no doubt in my mind we would have increased the number of women in the House without term limits."[10]

TABLE 5.6   DIFFERENCES BETWEEN MALE AND FEMALE
CANDIDATES IN SELF-ASSESSMENT

ASSESSMENT CATEGORIES	MEN CANDIDATES MEAN SCORE	WOMEN CANDIDATES MEAN SCORE	STATISTICAL SIGNIFICANCE
Name Recognition in District (N = 530)	2.11	2.11	.990
Ability to Run Campaign (N = 529)	2.43	2.60	.012
Public Speaking Ability (N = 531)	2.45	2.55	.107
Support from Party in District (N = 528)	2.26	2.41	.065
Support from State Party (N = 521)	2.16	2.35	.045
Local Fundraising Ability (N = 529)	2.05	2.30	.003
PAC Fundraising Ability (N = 510)	2.01	2.32	.003
Ability to Finance Own Campaign (N = 526)	1.68	1.63	.561

Note: Self assessment scores were coded as: 1 = low, 2 = fair, 3 = high.
Source: Legislative Candidate Survey

Women, however, do appear more likely to take on a race for the state senate in term-limited states than in states without limits. This suggests that while the percentage of women serving in the lower chamber may not improve much because of term limits, women incumbents in the lower house may seize the opportunities term limits present to move to the upper chamber.

THE RECRUITMENT OF MINORITY CANDIDATES

Although the number of minorities serving in state legislatures has grown over the last two decades, they still constitute a small portion of all legislators. Political geography plays a critical role in explaining the presence or absence of minorities in the state legislature. Where there are few minorities, virtually none of them are found in the legislature. Conversely, where minorities constitute a substantial portion of the electorate, far more of them are elected to office.

There are not many meaningful demographic differences between African-American and white candidates for the state legislature.[11] African-American candidates tend to be somewhat younger than their white counterparts. Differences between the two groups on education and income levels are minute.

Candidate Profile

☑ **FRAN NATIVIDAD COLEMAN**, Democratic candidate for the Colorado House District 1, 1998

Fran Coleman is a Latina in the district encompassing southwest Denver, an older, mostly blue-collar area. While a Republican represented the district in recent years, it is a district targeted by the Democrats. The voter registration figures are split almost evenly among Democrats, Republicans, and Independents. The district is about 25 percent Hispanic. There is a mix of economic groups, but it is mostly middle class. Senior citizens comprise a significant portion of the district voters.

Fran recently retired from US West as a telecommunications specialist. She holds a B.A. degree from Loretta Heights College (a small Catholic school in Denver) and a masters degree from the University of Denver.

Although she had always voted, she was not actively involved in politics until 1985, when her son, who was a high school student at the time, worked on a local campaign. He talked her into accompanying him to a Democratic precinct caucus meeting. She soon became involved in several local races.

In 1991, she ran for the Denver city council. "I learned a lot and lost miserably." Although she had failed to be elected to office, Denver's mayor eventually appointed Fran to the City Corrections Board. This appointment was an important step in her political career, giving her some exposure to policymaking, and allowing her the chance to develop important contacts among civic activists.

In 1998, House District 1 was an open seat because the Republican incumbent could not run again because of Colorado's term limit law. "I was interested in running for this seat several times before, but the Republican incumbent was well liked and it seemed like suicide to run." But when term limits forced the seat to become open, she again contemplated making the race. In the spring of 1997, local Democratic officials started courting her for the position. She was reluctant to commit at that time because of pending ankle surgery, but in October she read a newspaper article about Colorado's extremely low spending per pupil for public education. "The education issue was finally what drove me to run."

Once Fran tossed her hat into the ring, she spent months telephoning local people asking them to back her. She thought this activity would help scare off a couple of potential primary opponents. During this period she attended a candidate-training institute conducted by the Southwest Voter Registration Project, a group dedicated to increasing the political influence of Hispanics. Fran claimed this training "was very helpful. It taught me a lot about in-the-trenches, down-to-earth, detailed stuff that you need to know in a campaign." Fran also learned a lot "on how to run and win" from the National Women's Political Caucus.

Fran did not run specifically as a Latina: "I ran as Fran Coleman and I just let people figure out my ethnicity. I did send out one Latino piece targeted to Latino registered voters. Otherwise, I was Fran Coleman, neighbor and citizen running to be House District 1's representative."

Democratic party organizations were very supportive of her campaign. By October, Fran had received $700 from the local party, $1,100 from the Democratic Majority Fund (the Colorado House Democratic Caucus Campaign), and $2,500 from the Denver County Democratic Party. She had about a half-dozen meetings with house Democratic legislative leaders.

Fran eventually spent $44,000 on the campaign. She raised $36,500, a considerable sum given the strict contribution limits imposed under Colorado's new campaign finance initiative. Nonetheless, on election night she had a debt of $7,500, a sum about which, she humorously noted, "I am going to try and stay calm."

When asked what she learned during the campaign, she responded, "The race at this level depends largely on volunteers." Unlike congressional or statewide races, there is not enough money to hire a full-time campaign manager in most state legislative races. Most candidates have to learn how to organize and run their own campaigns. Fran understood this very well, and she understood the importance of face-to-face campaigning at the state legislative level. As she noted, "The trick to winning was disciplined knocking on doors every day from April to November, for a minimum of two hours a day!"

Fran Coleman won her election with 52 percent of the vote.

The Fran Coleman material is reprinted with the permission of Fran Coleman.

The only notable demographic contrasts are on sex and political experience. Women constitute a higher percentage of African-American candidates than they do of white candidates. Fewer African-American candidates currently hold appointive or elective office than do white candidates, meaning that in many cases they bring less experience to the campaign and, as a result, stand less chance for success.

There are, however, differences of great consequence between the recruitment processes that bring African Americans and whites into the race. Although roughly the same percentages of the two groups say that they were nudged or pushed to run, African-American candidates report far fewer contacts with party officials than do white candidates (see Table 5.7). The differences are striking. Only 16 percent of African-American candidates, for example, report being encouraged to run by local party officials. In contrast, 48 percent of white candidates say local party leaders asked them to make the race. Similar disparate relationships are found with state party leaders, local elected officials, and legislative leaders. Party agents are not important recruiters in bringing African Americans to run for the state legislature. Instead, African Americans are much more likely than are white candidates to be urged to run by people from their churches, their neighborhoods, and their families. Potential African-American candidates emerge from different sorts of social networks than do their white counterparts.

African-American candidates are much more likely to mull over their races with neighbors and with people from their churches than are white

TABLE 5.7   DIFFERENCES IN RECRUITMENT CONTACTS,
BY RACE (MAJOR-PARTY CANDIDATES)

	AFRICAN-AMERICAN CANDIDATES ($N = 25$)	WHITE CANDIDATES ($N = 561$)
PARTY ENCOURAGEMENT TO RUN		
Local Party Officials*	16%	48%
State Party Officials*	16	34
Local Elected Officials	24	34
Legislative Leaders*	12	35
NONPARTY ENCOURAGEMENT TO RUN		
Church Members*	32%	12%
Neighbors*	40	22
Interest Groups	12	14
Co-workers	20	20
Service Organizations	12	14

*Difference is statistically significant at .05 or better.
Source: Legislative Candidate Survey

candidates (see Table 5.8). In turn, African Americans are much less apt than are their white counterparts to confer about their possible candidacies with various party officials. Again, the data we have available makes it appear that very different social networks from those motivating potential white candidates encourage the political candidacies of African Americans.

THE RECRUITMENT OF THIRD-PARTY CANDIDATES

Few third-party candidates get elected to the state legislature, but it is important to understand who these people are and why they enter the race. As the 1997 state legislative elections in Virginia demonstrate, third-party candidates are sometimes the only challengers to an incumbent. Control of the Virginia House of Delegates was at stake in that election and both Republicans and Democrats had everything to gain from vigorously contesting each and every race. Yet, more often than not, they were unable to even field a candidate. One or the other major party failed to have a candidate on the ballot in sixty of the one hundred House races. In eleven of those districts, minor-party candidates—representing the Virginia Reform party, the Green party, and independent candidacies—provided the voters with their only alternative to the major-party candidate. Indeed, in District 19, only an independent challenger and an independent incumbent were on the ballot.

TABLE 5.8   DIFFERENCES IN WHO CANDIDATES CONSULT
ABOUT CANDIDACY, BY RACE (MAJOR-PARTY CANDIDATES)

	AFRICAN-AMERICAN CANDIDATES (N = 25)	WHITE CANDIDATES (N = 561)
DISCUSSIONS WITH PARTY OFFICIALS		
Local Party Officials*	36%	71%
State Party Officials*	20	52
Local Elected Officials	32	53
Legislative Leaders*	24	54
DISCUSSIONS WITH NONPARTY GROUPS		
Family Members	84%	94%
Church Members	44	28
Neighbors	44	36
Interest Groups	16	20
Co-workers	48	49
Service Organizations	20	34

*Difference is statistically significant at .05 or better.
Source: Legislative Candidate Survey

The situation in Virginia was not unusual. In New Jersey, for example, the Conservative Party fielded candidates in many races in 1997. A few candidates also ran from other minor parties, such as the Reform, Natural Law, Green, and Socialist parties. In the 1998 elections for the California Assembly, third-party candidates were on the ballot in forty-nine of the eighty districts. In three of those districts, they were the only alternative to the incumbent. A candidate from the Green Party even won a California assembly seat in a 1999 special election.[12]

There are few demographic differences between major- and minor-party candidates (see Table 5.9). A greater percentage of minor-party candidates than major-party candidates are sixty years old or older. More minor-party candidates than major-party candidates have relatively little formal education and earn lower incomes. Virtually no African Americans, Hispanic Americans, or American Indians run on third-party tickets, but women constitute essentially the same percentage of third-party candidates as they do of the major parties. Finally, minor-party candidates are only slightly less rooted in their communities than are major-party candidates. Overall, candidates running under third-party labels look very much like the people running as Republicans and Democrats.

Do third-party candidates bring the same level of political experience to the campaign as major-party candidates do? Experience matters, of course, because it tends to lead to more successful candidacies. Both minor-party candidates and major-party candidates have been active in federal and state level campaigns (see Table 5.10 on page 112). But major-party candidates report far more activity in local elections than their third-party counterparts. Being better grounded in local politics advantages major-party candidates because it provides them more financial and personal contacts to draw on in their districts.

More important, major-party candidates are much more likely to currently hold appointive or elective office than are minor-party candidates. This gives them an enormous leg up on the campaign because holding office gives candidates a greater opportunity to make the sort of contacts that translate into increased campaign contributions. The fact that more major- than minor-party candidates have made previous runs for the legislature also works to their benefit.

Third-party candidates are more apt to be self-starters than are major-party candidates.[13] The differences are not vast, but those running under minor-party banners run on their own initiative to a greater degree. Almost half of them say running was their idea compared to only 14 percent who say the thought had not occurred to them.

Given that almost no elective offices in the United States are won by third-party candidates, it is not surprising to learn that very few, if any, third-party candidates are recruited to run by local elected officials or legislative leaders (see Table 5.11 on page 112 and Table 5.12 on page 113). There simply are too few of them to be an important source of encouragement. Instead,

CANDIDATE AGE	MAJOR-PARTY CANDIDATES ($N = 538$)	MINOR PARTY CANDIDATES ($N = 67$)
Under 30 years of age	5%	3%
30–39 years of age	18	24
40–49 years of age	29	24
50–59 years of age	30	18
60–69 years of age	15	24
70 years and over	3	8
EDUCATION	($N = 538$)	($N = 66$)
0–11 years	6%	12%
High school graduate	17	20
Some college	26	21
College graduate	41	39
Post graduate	10	8
INCOME*	($N = 389$)	($N = 64$)
Under $30,000	12%	36%
$30,000–$49,999	24	25
$50,000–$69,999	19	8
$70,000–$89,999	18	13
$90,000–$119,999	12	14
$120,000 and over	15	5
SEX	($N = 536$)	($N = 66$)
Male	78%	76%
Female	22	24
RACE AND ETHNICITY	($N = 530$)	($N = 65$)
White/Caucasian	93%	99%
African American	5	0
Hispanic American	1	1
American Indian	1	0
RESIDENCY	($N = 535$)	($N = 67$)
Two Years or Less	4%	3%
Three to Five Years	9	13
Six to Ten Years	11	19
More than Ten Years	76	64

*This question was not asked of candidates in Colorado and Washington.

Source: Legislative Candidate Survey

TABLE 5.10   POLITICAL EXPERIENCE LEVEL
OF MAJOR- AND MINOR-PARTY CANDIDATES

TYPE OF POLITICAL EXPERIENCE	MAJOR-PARTY CANDIDATES ($N = 538$)	MINOR PARTY CANDIDATES ($N = 67$)
Active or Very Active in:		
Federal Campaign	67%	63%
Statewide Campaign	65	62
Local Campaign	73	48
Held:		
Some Party Post	60	51
More than One Post	31	28
Currently Hold:		
Appointive Office	10	2
Elective Office	25	6
Ran for Legislature Before:		
In Primary Only	7	7
In General Election	17	7
Served on:		
State Legislative Staff	5	3
Congressional Staff	3	3
Both Staffs	1	0

Source: Legislative Candidate Survey

TABLE 5.11   DIFFERENCES IN MAJOR-PARTY AND MINOR-PARTY
CANDIDATE RECRUITMENT CONTACTS

	MAJOR PARTY CANDIDATES ($N = 538$)	MINOR PARTY CANDIDATES ($N = 67$)
PARTY ENCOURAGEMENT TO RUN		
Local Party Officials*	46%	24%
State Party Officials	33	43
Local Elected Officials*	34	0
Legislative Leaders*	33	0
NONPARTY ENCOURAGEMENT TO RUN		
Church Members	12%	12%
Neighbors	23	21
Interest Groups*	14	5
Co-workers*	19	6
Service Organizations*	18	8

*Difference is statistically significant at .05 or better.
Source: Legislative Candidate Survey

TABLE 5.12   DIFFERENCES IN WHO MAJOR-PARTY
AND MINOR-PARTY CANDIDATES CONSULT ABOUT CANDIDACY

	MAJOR PARTY CANDIDATES (N = 538)	MINOR PARTY CANDIDATES (N = 67)
DISCUSSIONS WITH PARTY OFFICIALS		
Local Party Officials*	69%	46%
State Party Officials	50	51
Local Elected Officials*	52	10
Legislative Leaders*	52	5
DISCUSSIONS WITH NONPARTY GROUPS		
Family Members*	93%	76%
Church Members	29	19
Neighbors	36	37
Interest Groups*	19	6
Co-workers*	49	30
Service Organizations	33	22

*Difference is statistically significant at .05 or better.
Source: Legislative Candidate Survey

what pressure there is to run on a third-party ticket comes from state party officials. A greater percentage of third-party candidates than major-party candidates report being pushed to run by officials from the state party. Among nonparty sources, neighbors and fellow churchgoers are as important a source of encouragement for third-party candidates to run as they are for major-party candidates. But major-party candidates report far more recruitment efforts on the part of co-workers and from all sorts of groups and organizations than do third-party candidates.

Local party leaders are far more important to major-party candidates than they are to minor-party candidates, though both groups equally discuss their candidacies with state party leaders. Republican and Democratic candidates consult a much wider range of people than do third-party candidates. To a much greater degree than their major-party counterparts, third-party candidates launch their efforts on their own initiative and with much less input from others.

CONCLUSION

Women, minority, and third-party candidates operate in different social and political networks. In many ways, they bring the same sorts of characteristics and experiences to a campaign as do other candidates. Almost none of them are political novices. Most are qualified to serve in office by any standard. Yet they find themselves being encouraged to run by different sorts of people and organizations and they have very different sorts of relationships with political party representatives than do most white males running on major-party tickets. This suggests that the means for electing a more diverse assortment of people to the state legislature are to be found in exploiting the different social networks in which people operate. Traditional recruitment mechanisms may be slow to find people from underrepresented groups to run for office.

NOTES

1. See Susan Carroll, *Women as Candidates in American Politics*, 2nd ed. (Bloomington: Indiana University Press, 1994), 133; and Robert Darcy, Susan Welch, and Janet Clark, *Women, Elections, and Representation*, 2nd ed. (Lincoln: University of Nebraska Press, 1994), 107.
2. The Legislative Candidate Survey found that 78 percent of male candidates were married but only 63 percent of women candidates were married. Women were much more likely (25 percent) to be divorced, separated, or widowed than were men (10 percent). Eleven percent of the men and women had never been married.
3. In our survey, none of the women candidates under the age of thirty had children, while 13 percent of the male candidates in that age group did. Similarly, among candidates between the ages of thirty and thirty-nine, 62 percent of the men had children at home, compared to 42 percent of the women. It is only among candidates in their forties, when children are apt to be older and more self sufficient, that parity is reached: 70 percent of male candidates and 77 percent of female candidates have children at home.
4. David Niven, *The Missing Majority: The Recruitment of Women as State Legislative Candidates* (Westport, Conn.: Praeger, 1998), 23. Also see Carroll, *Women as Candidates*, 36–39; and Darcy, Welch, and Clark, *Women, Elections, and Representation*, 69–70.
5. For a different point of view, see Niven, *The Missing Majority*.
6. Christie Vilsack as quoted in Staci Hupp, "Rally Gives Women a Push to Politics," *Des Moines Register*, 28 September 1999.
7. Ralph Wright, *All Politics Is Personal* (Manchester Center, Vt.: Marshall Jones Co., 1996), 64.
8. This contradicts David Niven's finding on party-leader bias against women candidates. See Niven, *The Missing Majority*. Why the divergence between the two studies on such an important finding? We can point to two important differences in the survey samples used in the studies. First, Niven surveyed potential candidates, while we surveyed those who had made the commitment to run. A reasonable assumption is that those potential candidates who perceive that party leaders are biased against them are less likely to make the decision to run. In other words, those who experienced or perceived the most bias are probably self-selected out of our target population (which is candidates, not potential candidates). This is an important point and is consistent with our previous suggestion that for many women, the threshold of candidacy is higher than it is for men. The second difference between the two studies is the states examined. Niven surveyed potential candidates

in four states: California, New Jersey, Ohio, and Tennessee, the same states looked at by Wahlke, Eulau, Buchanan, and Ferguson in their classic study of several decades ago. (See John Wahlke, Heinz Eulau, William Buchanan, and LeRoy Ferguson, *The Legislative System* (New York: John Wiley & Sons, 1962). This is not a very representative sample of state legislatures in the 1990s. The first three states are among the few generally considered to have professional legislatures and the fourth is a southern state. Women are least likely to serve in professional state legislatures and those in the South. On these points see Peverill Squire, "Legislative Professionalization and Membership Diversity in State Legislatures," *Legislative Studies Quarterly* 17 (1992: 69–79; Darcy, Welch, and Clark, *Women, Elections, and Representation*; and Sue Vandenbosch, "A Negative Relationship Between Religion and the Percentage of Women State Legislators in the United States," *Journal of Legislative Studies* 2 (winter 1996): 322–338. In contrast, our sample includes a broader mix of states by region and level of professionalization. Thus, while Niven may well be correct in his assessment that party elites pose a barrier to the candidacies of women in the states he studied, we are not convinced that his conclusions can be generalized beyond his sample of states. We do not, for example, find them plausible in Washington state or Colorado.

9. Susan J. Carroll and Krista Jenkins, "The Effect of Term Limits on the Representation of Women: An Analysis of Evidence from the 1998 Elections" (Paper presented at the 1999 Annual Meeting of the Western Political Science Association, Seattle), 14.

10. Maxine Berman as quoted in Kathy Barks Hoffman, "Term Limits May have Kept Women from Increasing Numbers in House," *Detroit Free Press*, 8 November 1998.

11. Unfortunately, we have too few minority respondents to our survey to say anything very definitive about minority recruitment patterns. We can, however, use our data to give some ideas about the similarities and differences in the ways white and African-American candidates are brought into the campaign. Although we have Hispanic Americans, Asian Americans, and American Indians in our survey, there were too few members of each of these groups for meaningful analysis.

12. She later switched her affiliation to Independent.

13. While 32 percent of the major-party candidates said it "was entirely my idea" to run, 46 percent of the minor-party candidates said so. Minor-party candidates were somewhat less likely (14 percent) than were major-party candidates (22 percent) to say they "had not seriously thought about running until someone else suggested it." The survey contains only twenty-eight minor-party candidates, however, and therefore the results must be interpreted with some caution.

6

CANDIDATES AND THE QUALITY OF CIVIC LIFE

Political participation has declined in the United States. It is especially difficult to get people to become active in politics, to campaign for candidates, to work within parties, to join organizations concerned about issues. This lack of participation is a general trend, not limited to political organizations. People are less likely to join and become active in all sorts of groups and organizations. It may not undermine our society very seriously if fewer people are joining bowling leagues, Rotary organizations, or local college alumni groups. But if fewer persons are devoting much time to political organizations and to groups concerned with public policy, our political system is weakened.

Running for any political office is a very demanding form of participation because it requires a heavy commitment of time and effort. Yet the political system needs the best possible participants. State legislatures occupy a very important position in the political system. Legislative office is often the first elected office that candidates have sought. State legislatures play an increasingly important role in public policymaking, and are far better equipped to perform this role than they were thirty years ago. The state legislature is also an important "farm system" for congressional and state offices.

This book is about nonincumbents because most are making their first attempt at public office and it is a difficult and important step to declare one's candidacy, to put oneself before the public in this way. It is a step very few Americans are willing to take. But the health of the republic is dependent on at least some people being willing to make this commitment. Our goal in this book has been to shed some light on these people, and on the processes by which they crossed the threshold from citizen to candidate. Along the way, we discovered a number of things about the candidates and their campaigns. Foremost is that the overwhelming majority are not "professional politicians." Instead, they are real people who are active in their communities, have an interest in politics, and, for a variety of reasons, cross the threshold to candidacy.

Second, there is a shortage of candidates. Many legislative seats appear to be safe for one party, and prospective candidates in the other party are often reluctant to engage in what amount to political suicide missions. Even in seats that do not appear to be safe for one party, there are often entrenched incumbents who work hard to keep their seats by developing political skills and paying close attention to the interests and needs of their constituents—thereby discouraging strong challengers from running, and getting reelected easily.

Political parties have the responsibility for recruiting candidates, and there is evidence that many of them are taking this responsibility more seriously than in the past—but still there are many uncontested races. Some parties may not be doing their job very well; but others are targeting close races, and leaving uncontested the races they do not think can be won. Parties have a difficult time because prospective candidates know that running for legislative office is tough, hard work. Candidates must raise money, and most despise doing so. Candidates are subject to criticism from their opponents. Campaigning is so time-consuming that candidates may have to neglect their jobs and their families.

One important reason why recruiting is difficult is that many potential candidates have discovered that, even if they win election, they will be taking on a job that is difficult, pressure-filled, and time-consuming. The large majority of state legislators are not well paid, and they must divide their time between work in the legislature and with their constituency, on the one hand, and earning a living from their regular job or profession, on the other—while squeezing in some time for their family. These problems and pressures, which often lead legislators to retire after a few terms, are similar to those faced by most persons elected to local office. Elected officials at the state and local level are acutely aware that the quality of their family life is often undermined by their job—one reason why it is particularly difficult to recruit women with small children at home to run for office. As one elected official in Seattle said when she quit because she had two small children: "No public service job is more important than being a parent."[1]

Legislators have become increasingly disturbed by the way the media covers legislatures. A large proportion believe that the media is becoming overly critical and confrontational and less accurate in its coverage of the legislature.[2] This negative media coverage may also help explain the cynical views that many citizens have about legislators. Legislators find that some constituents expect their representative to agree with them on all issues and assume that if they don't they must have "sold out" to some interest. All of these are factors that may discourage potential candidates from running.

What difference does it make if seats go uncontested? Most obviously, it affects voters who often have little incentive to vote in legislative races. Many feel they have no good choices available in an election because their party is running unappealing candidates; others have no choice at all because their party has no candidate running for the legislature.

Uncontested races are not only a symptom of weak party competition, but may also be a cause of it. If a party fails to contest a number of races, its supporters lose interest. They either stay home, or begin to vote for candidates of the other party, making competition even more lopsided. A party's failure to contest some legislative seats and to make a serious effort in more districts discourages potential candidates from running.

Yet some people do run. Those who run are likely to be middle-aged and well educated, to have above-average income, to have deep roots in the community, and to be active in community affairs. In these respects, they are similar to candidates running for Congress.

In many respects, however, new state legislative candidates are *not* like congressional candidates. A large majority of them are making their first run for legislative office, and most of them have never held any elective office. As they make their first attempt to win legislative office, most of them do not yet have progressive ambitions. They are not yet thinking about making a career in politics and perhaps moving up to Congress or to a statewide office. Some may have thought that, if elected, they would like to serve a number of terms in the legislature, but most are probably uncertain about how long they want to, or will be able to, serve in the legislature.

The kinds of persons who run for the legislature are not the ones who spend every evening sitting in front of the television set. Almost all of them have been actively involved in organizations and most have played some role in community affairs. They are likely to be interested in and rather well informed about local and state issues. Some of them have been actively involved in controversies over particular issues, whether these are taxes, schools, the environment, or women's rights.

Some of these candidates have been active in politics, working in campaigns, and in some cases running for—or even winning—other offices, such as the school board. Some of them have been waiting for the right moment to run for the legislature, such as the absence of an incumbent in the race. Some are primarily interested in issues and run for the legislature in an effort to play a more direct role in changing public policy. And some candidates who have been active in their party decide to run because no one else seems willing to run for a seat held by the other party. These candidates are particularly interesting because they usually realize that the odds are against them in trying to win a seat that appears secure for the other party. But they run nonetheless, often simply to offer a choice to the voter.

The proportion of candidates who are female or members of racial or ethnic minorities is growing fairly slowly and unevenly from state to state. Women who run for the legislature are often motivated by concern over policy issues, and some may believe that it is important to have more female legislators. They often have a more difficult job than men in reconciling their commitment to campaigning and legislative service with their family responsibilities. Currently, women do not usually face the larger obstacles to candidacy that existed a generation ago when party organizations seemed to give them little support. But they are more likely to need encouragement from party leaders or others to run for office. Therefore, much of the burden for recruiting women legislative candidates rests on the party leadership and on groups that are trying to increase the proportion of women in public office.

In recent years, legislative party leaders have become much more active in recruiting some candidates and providing them with campaign assistance. They have learned what kinds of persons make good candidates. These include candidates who are both willing and able to work hard, devote huge amounts of time to campaigning, raise money relentlessly, and dedicate themselves to the campaign. They must have "the fire in the belly."

Party leaders are realistic about the problems of recruiting and finding the right person. They know that those they recruit to run often need advice and tangible assistance to be effective candidates, and they can and do provide financing. But party leaders can not always control the nomination and discourage a poorer candidate from entering the primary, particularly in districts where the party has a realistic chance of winning.

The parties usually focus their recruiting efforts and aid on candidates in close races, trying to hold the seats that are at risk and capture others that appear winnable—identifying such districts by carefully studying voting records. Such a targeting strategy makes political sense for parties that are trying to win enough seats to gain or maintain a majority in the legislative chamber, but this strategy often leaves many seats uncontested.

Every legislative campaign is different, but outside a few states like California, legislative campaigning is very different from a congressional campaign. Most state legislative candidates can not hire high-priced managers and consultants. Running commercials on television, or sometimes even on radio, is usually prohibitively expensive and very inefficient because legislative districts are small and rarely coincide with the media market area. Candidates find that the voting public usually does not pay much attention to legislative races. Campaigning door-to-door may be very effective, but it is also very time-consuming, even in modest-sized districts.

To have a reasonable chance of winning in a close district, candidates need name recognition and a base of support from previous activities in the community. They may have been an active member of a large church, a little league coach, or the president of a civic club. They may have been a successful businessperson in a large company. If they have worked in a previous political campaign, they have not only gained valuable experience but developed contacts with large numbers of persons willing to work in campaigns.

Candidates should know their district well enough to recognize where Democratic and Republican voters are clustered, and thus where they have the best chance of winning votes. They need to put together a network of persons and groups with which they have been identified. These may be business leaders, or persons active in labor unions, or members of their church or neighborhood organization, for example. These may be persons who share their general viewpoint on issues and with whom they worked on civic projects, such as improving schools or cleaning up the environment. They also have to find ways of developing a position on issues that is acceptable to at least some of the groups that are politically strong in the district, such as teachers' organizations.

In order to run a race that is at least somewhat competitive, the candidate must somehow raise enough money to run the kind of campaign that is typical for the district. In a small district, it may not cost too much for one mailing, some yard signs, and a few newspaper ads. The larger the district, of course, the greater the cost of campaigning and the greater the likelihood that the candidate who is able to raise the most money will win.

Candidates who work hard and run credible races, regardless of whether they win or lose, are likely to have a better chance of winning in the next electoral cycle. Although some candidates become discouraged after one losing effort, some of them emerge from the campaign saying that, having learned from their experience, they might like to run again. Many believe that they could do better next time. Even the losers often say that they have enjoyed some aspects of the campaign, such as meeting people and ringing doorbells across the district.

A number of changes have occurred in legislative elections in the last twenty years. It is more difficult today to defeat incumbents because they are more experienced, have more political skills and more staff assistance. They work much harder to stay in touch with their constituents and provide services for them. They serve longer terms because the job is more important, more interesting, and more time-consuming.

In about one-third of the states, term limits imposed by voters through state initiatives are forcing legislators to leave after a few terms, creating more opportunities for new candidates. Political parties will have to adjust their recruiting strategies to fit the new rules. Competition is greater in open seats, and prospective candidates may be less willing to run against an incumbent in a particular election, since the incumbent will be forced to step down two or four years later.

Because of Republican party growth in the southern states, most states have closer two-party competition than twenty years ago. But, even in highly competitive states, lots of districts are fairly safe for one party or the other. Districts that are not safe for a political party may be safe for an incumbent, and might become more competitive if the incumbent did not run again.

While many congressional races are becoming high tech, with greater use of television and modern techniques for communicating, most of these innovations are very expensive. Most legislative races, outside the biggest states and districts, are much simpler, less high tech, and much less expensive. The techniques of legislative campaigning have not changed very much, although almost any campaign can make effective use of computers, web sites, copying machines, and faxes. The cost of legislative races is growing, almost inevitably, but not consistently from state to state, and not very fast in some states. In most legislative campaigns, much still depends upon a candidate's experience in politics, ability to communicate, willingness to work hard, and ability to build an organization.

One more change that is occurring, more rapidly in some states than others, is that the legislature is becoming more representative of the diverse groups in the state. In some states, there have been dramatic gains in the number of women running for the legislature, and the number winning; in other states, there is very little change. In states with larger proportions of racial and ethnic minorities, there have been some gradual gains in the proportion of minority candidates and the number who win.

What are the implications of all this for the voter? Does the campaign process help the voters to know the candidates well and understand the issues? In close elections, particularly if both candidates are well known at the start of the race, voters have a chance to learn something about both of them. But legislative races are usually not high-visibility contests, partly because candidates can not afford expensive means of communicating, partly because voters are paying more attention to races for president, governor, and senator. There is no obvious way to make voters pay more attention to such races even though those elected to the legislature participate in deciding issues that may have a major impact on the citizens. The cost of communicating with voters and the lack of public interest in legislative races make it difficult for nonincumbent candidates to develop issues that will help them get elected. Incumbents, on the other hand, have many opportunities during their term of office to explain to constituent groups and interests what they are accomplishing in the legislature on their behalf. At a time when the role of state legislatures and the issues they deal with continue to grow in importance, it is becoming less likely that voters will have a meaningful choice in legislative elections and will be well enough informed about the race to make a wise choice.

We began this book by noting that many legislative races are uncontested. What if they held an election and only one person's name was on the ballot? It already happens in over one-third of the state legislative elections in the United States. This does not make for a healthy democracy.

Is there a solution to the problem? There are many proposals: campaign finance reform, changes in the electoral system itself, term limits to break the power of incumbency, higher legislative salaries to attract more and perhaps better qualified candidates. These are all issues worthy of public discussion and debate. But our aim in this book has been somewhat different. It is our hope that readers will begin to see candidates as real people who undertake a difficult but vitally important role and will come to appreciate the effort that candidates put forth in running for election.

NOTES

1. Linda Keene, "Running from Public Office," *Seattle Times*, 21 November 1999, A1, A18.
2. Gary F. Moncrief, Joel A. Thompson, and Karl T. Kurtz, "The Old Statehouse Ain't What It Used To Be," *Legislative Studies Quarterly* 21 (1996): 57–72.

INDEX